Do-It-Yourself Decorating
Step-by-Step
Window Treatments

Jenny Plucknett

Meredith® Books

Des Moines, Iowa

Contents

First Decisions 4

Choosing a style   6

Choosing fabrics   8

Linings, kits, and accessories   10

Tracks, poles, and rods   12

Before You Begin: Curtains 14

Curtain style, size, and shape   16

Heading styles   18

Installing curtain tracks and poles   20

Buying curtain fabric   22

Cutting out and pattern matching   24

Making Curtains 26

Unlined curtains   28

Detachable linings   30

Sheer curtains   32

Café curtains   34

Lined curtains   36

Interlined curtains   38

Scalloped headings   40

Curtain Dressing 42

Classic tiebacks   44

Creative tiebacks   46

Simple valances   48

haped valances   50

Draped headings   52

wag and tails   54

Before You Begin: Blinds   56

Blind styles   58

Hanging blinds   60

Calculating quantities   62

Making Blinds   64

Roller blind   66

Roman blind   68

Festoon blind   70

Austrian blind   72

Sewing Techniques   74

Essential sewing kit   76

Hand stitches   78

Seams and hems   80

Corners   82

Piping and ruffles   84

Borders   86

Finishing touches   88

Patterns   90

Glossary   92

Index   94

Acknowledgments   96

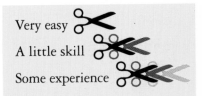

Very easy
A little skill
Some experience

First Decisions

In the same way that a room's color scheme will affect the choice of fabric, the style, position, and shape of a window will dictate the type of window treatment that will be most effective. Yet, there still are many other factors to consider.

This chapter provides ideas for window treatments for a range of window shapes and situations. You'll learn about the wide range of fabrics and linings available and their suitability for different types of curtains or blinds. And you'll receive an overview of alternative hanging systems and the kits and accessories that are available.

This chapter contains

Choosing a style	6
Choosing fabrics	8
Linings, kits, and accessories	10
Tracks, poles, and rods	12

Choosing a style

You have dozens of options when it comes to choosing a style of window treatment. In addition to considering the window's location and the room's use, color scheme, and furnishings, think about whether you want to emphasize or hide the style and shape of the window and frame or screen the view.

▲ Overscaled, floor-draping curtains and a decorative top edge can add drama to ordinary windows. A simple way to provide interest is to wrap or cover the pole with coordinating fabric. To increase the window size visually, attach the hanging system above or outside the window frame.

◄ To give more importance to small windows, make an oversized curtain and drape it to one side with a tieback.

▲ Windows with an interesting view look best with a simple treatment that frames the outlook.

▲ Recessed windows can be treated in several ways. Hang floor-length curtains outside the recess or fit curtains or blinds inside. Combining both treatments in coordinating fabrics can create a lavish, rich effect suitable for formal settings.

▲ Kitchens and bathrooms need treatments that are easy to clean and care for. Roller or Roman blinds keep fabric out of the way of work areas and surfaces. If you need daytime privacy, consider a half-window café curtain or flat panel tied to a rod.

▲ Bay windows often look best with a simple treatment that shows off the decorative shape. Roman blinds, made to cover each window independently, can be used as sun shades when necessary. Add curtains outside the bay for a more formal or romantic look.

▲ Windows without a view can be successfully screened with sheer blinds. Consider festoon or Roman blinds in a translucent fabric. Or simply hang two large panels on a single rod, and pull the top panel to one side.

Choosing fabrics

When buying curtain fabric, consider the weight of the fabric and how it drapes, it resistance to fading and soiling, and the ease with which it can be cleaned.

TYPES OF FIBERS

Fabrics may be produced from natural or synthetic fibers or a mixture of the two. Natural fibers—which include cotton, linen, silk, and wool—are resistant to dust and dirt and clean well, although some can fad and shrink when washed. Pure linen and silk fabrics wrinkle easily. Synthetic fibers may be totally synthetic, such as polyester, nylon, and acrylic. Or they may be derived from plant material that is chemically treated, such as viscose. Synthetic fibers usually are easy to wash, crease- and shrink-resistant, and tough. However, because they attract dust and dirt, they require more frequent cleaning than natural fibers. Many fabrics combine synthetic and natural fibers, thus benefitting from the advantages of each.

Lace

Lace can be made from cotton, synthetic fibers, or a mixture of the two. The ornamental openwork patterns make it ideal for use as a decorative screen.

Calico

A cheap, firm, unbleached cotton, calico drapes well but is prone to shrinkage and creasing. It is effective for lavish window treatments.

Voile

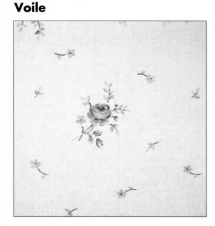

Voile can be 100-percent cotton, polyester, or a polyester/cotton blend. Available in solid colors and printed motifs, it is ideal for festoon blinds and curtains.

Synthetic sheer

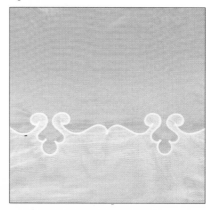

Sheer fabrics mad from synthetic fibers are tough and easily washed A wide range of widths is available, and some sheers come with a decorative edging and a casing.

Printed cotton

Most cottons are sturdy and drape well. Lightweight polyester/cotton blends, which are strong and fade resistant, are suitable for smaller lined curtains and blinds.

Muslin

This is an open-weave cotton that's usually white or cream. It drapes well and is inexpensive, which makes it ideal for full curtains.

Woven cotton

Medium-weight, tightly woven cotton is best for blinds. However, for use as roller blinds, the fabric must first be stiffened.

Gingham

This lightweight cotton or polyester/cotton fabric comes with a woven check. An attractive, simple fabric, it's ideal for kitchens and bathrooms.

Linen union

Made from a blend of cotton and linen, often with nylon added, this fabric is more common in Europe than in the United States.

Velvet

A deep-pile fabric made from silk, cotton, or synthetic fibers, velvet requires special care. Its pile must always run in the same direction.

Linings, kits, and accessories

A curtain lining protects the main curtain fabric and improves the way it hangs. Lining fabrics tend to wear out before the main fabrics, so invest in the best quality you can afford.

For additional insulation, thickness, and weight, include an interlining—an extra layer of material sandwiched between the main fabric and the lining.

Check fabric shops and home-improvement stores for kits that will make window treatments quicker and easier to produce. You'll also find a range of special accessories that add a professional touch to the finished effect.

LINING FABRICS

Cotton sateen

This is a quality lining fabric. Available in a range of colors, cotton sateen comes in a standard 48-inch width and a wider 54-inch width. Solid colors of easy-care polyester/cotton fabric and cotton poplin also are suitable choices.

Blackout lining

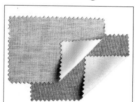

This polyester/cotton lining, designed to block light, may be more commonly used in Europe than in the United States.

Thermal lining

There are two types of thermal lining: a cotton/acrylic blend that comes in white and ecru and a more expensive alternative with an aluminum coating.

INTERLININGS

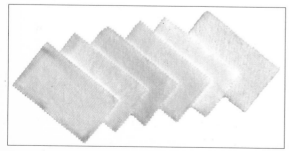

Interlinings add body and insulation to curtains and valances. One common interlining for full-length draperies is a 100-percent-cotton flannel with nap on both sides. For lightweight and medium-weight fabrics, choose a loosely woven, even-weave 100-percent cotton. You'll also find interlinings of various fiber blends. If you're in doubt, ask for guidance at the fabric store.

KITS

Blinds

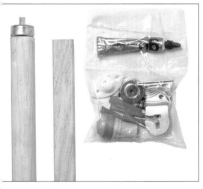

Kits for making blinds are available in a range of sizes. They contain all you need to make a blind with your own fabric, including the track and hardware.

Eyelets

These kits let you produce interlaced and tied headings easily. You can buy eyelets (or grommets) and an eyelet tool at most fabric and crafts stores.

Tab-tops

The kits include iron-on buckram strips, pins, butterfly clips, and button shapes for covering with your own fabric. No sewing is necessary.

ACCESSORIES

Pelmet former

This self-adhesive plastic sheet has pelmet (valance) shapes preprinted on the backing paper. It's more readily available in Europe than in the United States.

Cord tidy

Designed to hold heading cords neatly after they've been pulled up to gather curtains or blinds, tidies are often used in England.

Hook-and-loop fastening tape

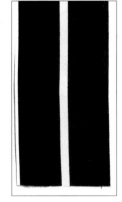

A simple way to attach lightweight fixed curtains, Roman blinds, valances, and bed coronets, this tape allows easy removal for cleaning.

Lead weights

Stitched into curtain hems, lead weights help the curtains hang well. They are available in lightweight, medium-weight, and heavyweight lengths and in button shapes.

Curtain clips

Available in a wide range of styles, clips let you hang lightweight curtains, blinds, and valances quickly and easily.

Tracks, poles, and rods

Hanging systems for window treatments fall into two main categories: those that are hidden behind the treatment and those that form a decorative part of the overall effect. Tracks, which usually are less expensive than poles, fall into the first category. They can be shaped to go around a curve in a bay window or to fit neatly into a recess. Wood, brass, and iron poles form an integral part of the finished look. Although some types of rods can be mitered or bent for curved windows, most poles are best for flat window frames.

CURTAIN TRACKS

Suitable for lightweight to medium-weight curtains, curtain tracks generally are made of plastic and come

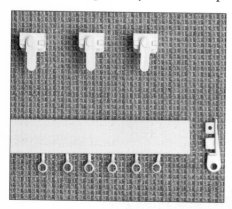

in a wide range of lengths with mounting brackets, slip-on hooks for hanging curtains, and end-stops to hold hooks on the track.

Some tracks have curtain hooks with rings below them to take curtains with detachable linings.

Alternatives include expandable steel track and track systems with integral cording, allowing the curtains to be drawn from one side.

VALANCE RAILS

Valance rails are available as a single rail that holds a valance on its own or as a combined track and rail,

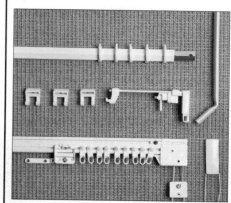

where curtains hang from the track behind and the valance hooks over the rail in front.

BLIND TRACK

This is designed for use with Austrian and festoon blinds. Apart from the curtain track (with curtain hooks and cord tidies to take the blind's pulled-up

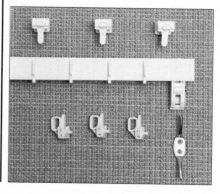

vertical cords), it has cord holders that slide into position above each length of vertical tape to take the pulley cords and a cord lock at one end.

WOOD POLES

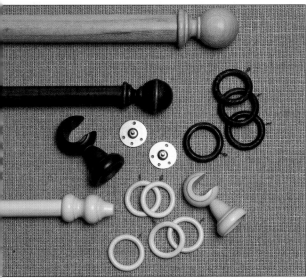

Poles are available in a range of thicknesses and a variety of finishes, from natural to stained or painted. Some kits include matching end finials, rings, and wall brackets. Often, however, you'll have to buy these pieces separately.

IRON POLES

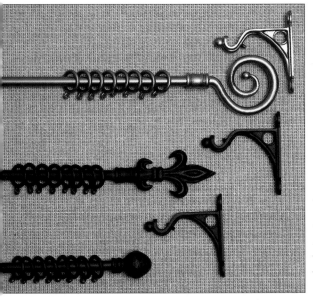

Slender and strong, iron poles may be designed with simple curved ends or ornately decorative finials and come with wall brackets and rings. Plain iron rods can be used to hold tab-, rod-pocket-, and tie-on-style curtains that don't require rings.

BRASS POLES

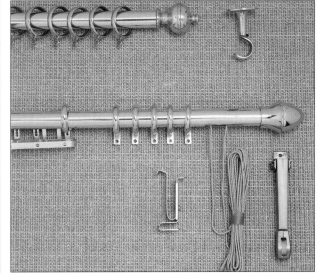

Brass or brass-finished poles come in a wide range of thicknesses and in some cases are expandable. In other instances, the front view of the pole hides runners for hanging the curtains and an integral cording set.

STRETCH WIRES AND TENSION RODS

This type of system usually is used for sheer and café curtains that remain across the window. The wire or rod slips through a casing in the top of the curtain and is then attached to the frame with hooks. Tension rods are designed to grip the inside wall of the recess. Or they may rest in end sockets that screw into the walls or window frame.

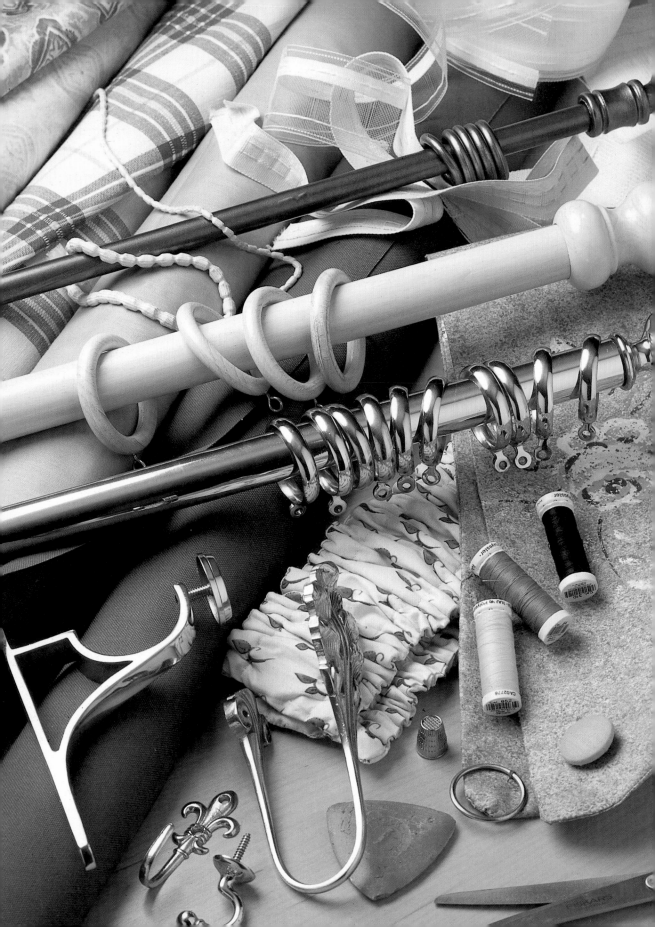

Before You Begin: Curtains

Once you have chosen the style of window treatment you want to make and the type of hanging system you'll be using, you can buy fabric and begin assembling the curtains.

This chapter explains how to install the hanging system, measure the window, and calculate the amount of fabric that will be required. It provides a framework for achieving professional-looking results with tips on what to look for when buying fabric, how to calculate fabric quantities for different types of heading tape, and most importantly, how to cut out and join fabric so the patterns match.

This chapter contains

Curtain style, size, and shape	16
Heading styles	18
Installing curtain tracks and poles	20
Buying curtain fabric	22
Cutting out and pattern matching	24

Curtain style, size, and shape

When choosing a window treatment, consider not only the overall style that you want to create, but practical issues, such as curtain length. Curtains usually are made in one of four lengths, depending on the window style, shape, and position.

◄ A large window in a large room can accept an elaborate treatment that includes a decorative topping of a valance or swags and tails. In a small room, bold fabric patterns and lavish treatments can be overpowering, so choose fabrics that blend with the surrounding decorations; add interest with complementary borders, cords, or fringes.

FLOOR-DRAPED CURTAINS
Extra-long curtains that puddle or pool generously on the floor are popular now. A drape of about 12 inches usually is adequate.

◄ To make a small window appear larger, attach the hanging system above and to the sides of the window.

Sheer curtains can be light, airy, and simple or sumptuously gathered, crossed, and tied back as shown here. Also consider lace roller blinds, organdy festoon blinds, or Roman blinds.

To create the illusion of width on tall, narrow windows, use a valance in a complementary fabric, and add a wide border of the same fabric below the window.

FLOOR-LENGTH CURTAIN

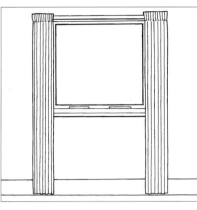

Measure from the track to the floor, then subtract ½ inch so the curtain stops just above the floor. This reduces wear along the hem edge.

ABOVE A RADIATOR

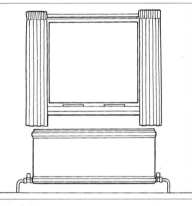

If you have a radiator immediately below a window, make short curtains to avoid blocking the heat. Measure from the track to the top of the radiator, then subtract ½ inch for a suitable curtain length.

RECESSED WINDOW

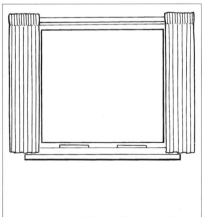

A recessed window with a wide sill requires curtains that stop at sill level. Measure from the track, pole, or rail to the sill and subtract ½ inch for the finished curtain length. For curtains hung outside the recess, measure from the track to the sill and add from 2 to 5 inches so the curtains hang just below the sill.

Heading styles

Fabric stores offer a wide range of ready-made tapes for making curtains, valances, and gathered blinds. The style of heading tape you choose will affect the amount of fabric you need, the way the fabric drapes, and the overall effect of the curtain.

Most wider tapes can be attached so the heading hides the track; or the curtains can be hung from rings on a pole.

PENCIL-PLEAT TAPE

The tape for pencil pleats is stiff, and when pulled up, it forms slim, straight pleats that are close together. Narrower widths are better suited to shorter curtains and valances; use the widest width for full-length curtains.

Tape widths available: 1½ inches, 3 inches, and 5½ inches, plus a 2½-inch-wide translucent tape for nets and sheer fabrics

Fabric requirement: 2½ times the track, pole, or rod length

GATHERED-HEADING TAPE

This tape is narrower and usually placed just below the top edge of the curtain. It is used either to make a traditional gathered heading or to form clustered gathers. It's best for headings that will be covered by a valance. Special tape for nets and sheers also is available.

Widths available: 1 inch (standard tape) and ⅜ inch (net tape)

Fabric requirement: 1½ to two times the track, pole, or rod length

TRIPLE-PLEAT TAPE

To create a fanned pleat, use triple-pleat heading tape. When the cords are pulled up, this tape forms fans of triple pleats evenly spaced along the curtain heading.

Widths available: 1½ inches, 3¼ inches, and 5½ inches

Fabric requirement: twice the track, pole, or rod length

LINING TAPE

This is designed for a detachable lining. The tape has an opening along the lower edge to receive the top raw edge of the curtain lining. The stitching traps the lining inside. The tape is gathered to fit the curtain, then hooks are added.

BOX-PLEAT TAPE

The tape forms closely spaced box pleats. This type of heading is designed as a decorative finish for a valance or curtain that remains in a fixed position.
Width available: 3 inches
Fabric requirement: three times the track length

SMOCKED-FINISH TAPE

A smocked heading forms a decorative finish for valances and curtains and also is ideal for fine nets and sheers. When the tape is pulled up, it creates an effect like smocking.
Width available: 3 inches
Fabric requirement: 2½ times the track, pole, or rod length

GOBLET-PLEAT TAPE

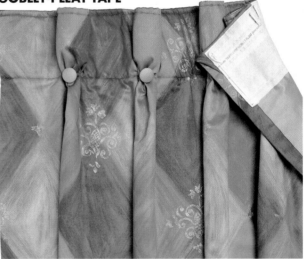

Until recently, goblet pleats had to be constructed by hand. Now you can buy a tape that produces large goblet-shaped pleats with three smaller pleats falling from the stem point.
Width available: 5½ inches
Fabric requirement: 2¼ times the track or pole length

Installing curtain tracks and poles

Brackets hold both curtain tracks and poles in place. In most cases, these come as part of the kit, along with the appropriate screws.

How you install the track or pole depends on the type of wall or window frame to which you'll be attaching it. Wooden window frames, masonry walls, drywall, and plaster require different types of hardware.

INSTALLING SCREWS

Wood

First mark the position for the screw with an awl or a hammer and nail. To make inserting the screw easier, drill a pilot hole (slightly smaller than the screw size) before driving the screw home with a screwdriver.

Drywall

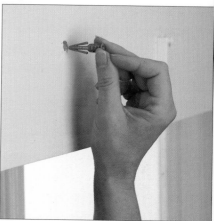

Partition walls are often made of drywall attached to wooden studs with a cavity behind the drywall. To drive a screw into a stud, use the same method as for wood.

If you have to install the screw in the wall between the studs, use a special wall plug with a toggle; the toggle opens to form an anchor against the back of the drywall as you tighten the screw. Drill a hole to fit the wall plug, push it though, then drive the screw home. This type of attachment is only suitable for lightweight curtains.

Masonry walls

To install a screw in a masonry wall, first fit a wall plug into the hole. Use a masonry bit to drill the hole. The drill bit, screw, and wall plug should all match in size. Make a starting hole by turning the drill by hand, then drill the hole to the length of the wall plug. Insert the plug, and drive the screw home with a screwdriver.

CURTAIN TRACKS

Most curtain tracks can be attached either to the ceiling or to the wall. To attach a track to the ceiling, screw the brackets into a joist to make sure they can bear the weight. When installing the track just above a window with a concrete lintel above it, you probably will need to attach the track to a furring strip. In this case make sure the strip is longer than the lintel so you can drill into the wall beyond it.

Once the strip is fixed in place, it can be painted or papered. Then the track brackets can be screwed to it.

CURTAIN POLES

Curtain pole brackets are attached in the same way as track brackets. The brackets that come with the pole are designed to be placed 3 to 5 inches in from the pole end; one ring is placed in the space remaining at each end.

1 To position the brackets, first draw a line along the wall where the track is to be attached. Use a level to make sure that the line is horizontal. Check the manufacturer's guidelines for spacing the brackets, then mark the position for each bracket along the line, placing the first and last brackets about 2 inches in from the ends of the track.

2 Once all the brackets are in place, attach the track to them, then slide on the gliders and position the end stops. With some tracks, the hooks are first attached to the curtain and then slipped into the gliders. With others, the hooks and gliders are combined, and the curtain heading is slipped over these.

Buying curtain fabric

Before buying fabric, you must calculate the precise amount of fabric you'll need. In addition to window measurements, consider the hanging system, the heading tape to be used, and most importantly, the size of the pattern repeat on your chosen fabric. When you're choosing fabric, be sure to check the label for fiber content, recommended uses, and cleaning instructions.

BUYING TIPS

- **Color matching:** Take a color chart, carpet samples, and fabric swatches with you to check color compatibility.
- **Color checks:** Take home a small sample or pattern repeat of the chosen fabric to check the effect of the fabric in both daylight and artificial light.
- **Crease resistance:** Crease a corner of the fabric in your hand to see whether the fabric remains crumpled.
- **Shrinkage:** If you intend to wash your curtains, buy preshrunk fabric; or ask the fabric-store clerk about the amount of shrinkage, and buy extra yardage accordingly.
- **Pattern repeat:** Check the length of the pattern repeat and add this to each curtain length when calculating the amount of fabric required.
- **Fabric flaws:** Before the fabric is cut, check the length carefully for flaws; make sure the pattern has been printed straight and follows the fabric grain.
- **Safety and wear:** Use flame- and stain-resistant fabrics for children's rooms. Or apply flame- and stain-retardant finishes as a spray after making the curtains.

PATTERN REPEAT

If you choose a fabric with a design that needs to be matched across the width, you will need to allow extra fabric. A salesperson at the fabric store can check the pattern repeat and help you calculate the amount of extra fabric you'll need. A bold motif looks best if the bottom of the design sits on the lower hem edge, so allow extra fabric to accommodate this, too. Valances in the same fabric as the curtain or blind also will look better if the pattern matches.

MEASURING AND CALCULATING FABRIC QUANTITIES

Before you can calculate the required fabric, you'll need to decide on the track or pole and the heading tape you need to achieve the desired finished effect. Then follow the simple procedure below to work out your fabric requirements.

CALCULATING HEADING TAPE

Measurement W (see Step 3, below) gives you the length of heading tape needed. Add 4 to 8 inches to the length to allow for pleat positions and for pulling the cord ends out.

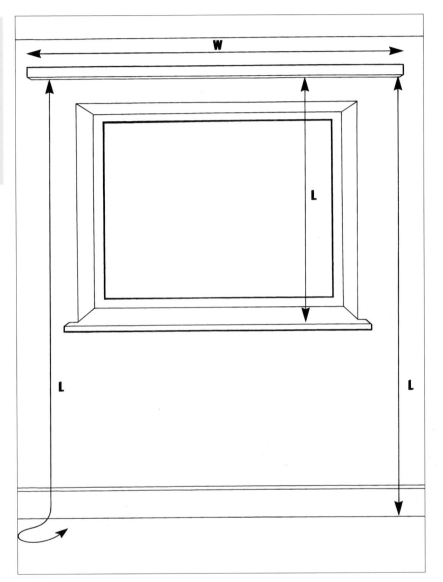

1 Choose your hanging system (see pages 12 and 13), decide on the position, and measure the length that you require. Fix the track or pole in place (see pages 20 and 21) to ensure the accurate measurement of the finished fabric length.

2 Decide on the curtain length (see pages 16 and 17) and measure this distance from the track or pole. Add about 3 inches for the heading (more for a deep heading tape) and about 6 inches for a hem allowance. This measurement will be L (length).

3 Select a heading style (see pages 18 and 19) and check the fabric fullness required—usually between 1½ to three times the track length. Measure the length of the track or pole and multiply this length by the fabric fullness, adding 2 inches for each side hem. If the track overlaps at the center add an additional 12 inches. This measurement will be W (width).

4 To calculate the number of fabric widths required, divide measurement W by the width of the chosen fabric. If the measurement falls between two widths, round the number up to the next full width.

5 Multiply the number of widths required by the length L to find the amount of fabric required.

Cutting out and pattern matching

Be careful when you cut out the fabric—a mistake could prove expensive. It's well worth the extra time it takes to double-check your calculations and measurements before taking scissors to the fabric. Once the first length of fabric has been cut, use it as a guide for cutting the rest of the lengths needed for the curtain width.

WORK AREA

If possible, set up a separate working area so you don't have to put away your materials every time you stop working. Or use the largest open area you have.

Sewing machine: Place the machine on a solid surface that's well lit by natural light. A working light is a useful addition, too.

Iron and ironing board: Leave these set up and ready for use at all times during the sewing process. Regular pressing ensures a professional finish.

Work table: Use a large, rectangular table for laying and cutting out lengths of fabric prior to pinning, basting, and stitching. Alternatively, use the largest floor area available and cover it with plastic or old sheeting.

PREPARING FABRIC

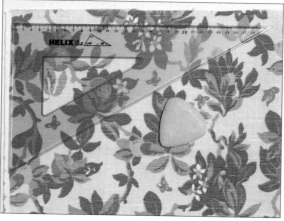

Before cutting, press the fabric and make sure the top edge is straight with the grain of the fabric. To do this, lay out the fabric on a hard, flat surface. Place a triangle, T-square, or other right-angled object on the top edge to get a right angle. Extend the top edge of the right angle with a yardstick and draw a line along it with tailor's chalk. Cut along the top edge following the drawn line. Remove the selvages down each side.

PLAIN FABRIC

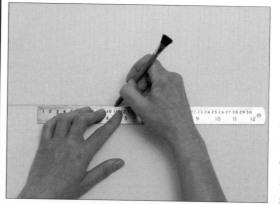

Carefully measure the first length and make a mark with tailor's chalk on each side edge of the fabric. Connect the marks, then cut along the line. Use this length as a guide for cutting out the other lengths required to make up each curtain.

ATTERNED FABRIC

lan carefully before cutting out patterned fabrics. On curtains (and festoon and Austrian blinds), the wer edge of the design should sit on the finished lower hem edge. Also, the pattern should match up rtically from the curtain to a valance heading.

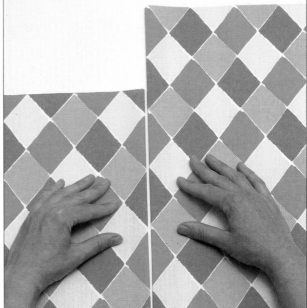

1 Carefully measure out the first length, making sure that the pattern is correctly positioned nd allowing for hem turnings below the lower pattern edge. Make a mark with tailor's chalk on ach side edge of the fabric. Connect the marks nd cut out the length.

2 To match the pattern across the widths, place the cut length on a flat surface and position the uncut fabric beside it. Move the cut length up and down until the pattern matches exactly with the pattern on the uncut fabric. Mark and cut the next length. Repeat, using this method to cut out all of the required lengths.

OINING LENGTHS

f you need to join half widths to nake up the required width of fabric or a curtain or blind, position the artial widths on the outer side of ach curtain; that way, they'll be ess noticeable.

Before cutting the fabric length, be ure to match motifs if you're using atterned fabric. Fold the fabric ength in half lengthwise and secure t with pins, then cut along the fold. titch one panel to the outer side of ach curtain, matching motifs.

Making Curtains

The type of window treatment you choose plays an important part in creating the overall look of a room. But the room also influences the curtain style. In kitchens and bathrooms, for example, unlined curtains are ideal because they are easy to wash. In a room that lacks privacy or has an unattractive view, sheers and café curtains can screen the outdoors while still allowing sunlight into the room.

Once decisions about the style of curtain and the hanging system have been made, you can begin stitching. This chapter contains the techniques for making a variety of the most popular types of curtains, from simple unlined ones to more complex interlined draperies.

This chapter contains

Unlined curtains	28
Detachable linings	30
Sheer curtains	32
Café curtains	34
Lined curtains	36
Interlined curtains	38
Scalloped headings	40

Unlined curtains

Unlined curtains are easy to make. They're a practical choice for kitchens, bathrooms, or a child's playroom, especially if they are made from an easy-care washable fabric, such as a polyester/cotton blend.

Each curtain is formed from single or joined widths of fabric, with hems at the sides and lower edge and heading tape along the top. If partial widths are needed for the curtain size, attach these at the outer edge of each curtain.

MATERIALS: Lightweight to medium-weight furnishing fabric, matching thread, pencil-pleat heading tape, track or pole

FABRIC: To calculate the amount of fabric required, follow the instructions for measuring the window and calculating fabric quantities (see pages 22 and 23). You will need a length of curtain tape the width of each finished curtain, plus 4 inches to allow for positioning.

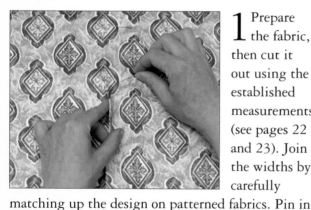

1 Prepare the fabric, then cut it out using the established measurements (see pages 22 and 23). Join the widths by carefully matching up the design on patterned fabrics. Pin in place to secure.

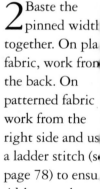

2 Baste the pinned width together. On plain fabric, work from the back. On patterned fabric work from the right side and use a ladder stitch (see page 78) to ensure the design matches exactly. Stitch widths together using flat-fell seams (see page 81).

3 To hem the sides, turn under ½ inch to the wrong side on each side and press, then fold under 1½ inches on each side, forming a double hem. Press and baste. Machine-stitch the hem in place or use a slip-stitch (see page 79).

4 Turn down the top edge of the fabric to the width of the heading tape and press. Position the top edge of the tape ¼ inch down from the folded top edge, covering the raw edge of the fabric. Allow a 2-inch tape overlap at each end. Pin the tape in position and baste to secure.

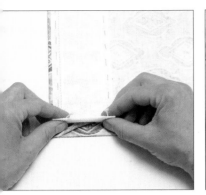

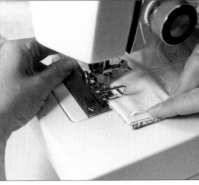

5 To neaten the tape ends, turn under the 2-inch overlap and baste in place as follows: On the edge where the curtains will meet (the leading edge), knot the cords, and then include them in the overlap. On the outer edge, pull the cords to the front of the tape so they are ready for gathering up.

6 Stitch the tape in place along the top and bottom edges, sewing in the same direction each time, then stitch across the ends. Make sure the stitching catches the cords on the leading edge to hold them in position, but do not catch the cords at the outer edge.

7 Before you stitch the hem, check the curtain length. Pull the cords in the heading tape and hang the curtains. Mark the hem and then remove the curtains. Press and baste a double hem in place. For a neat finish, miter the corners (see pages 82 and 83). Baste and stitch the hem.

Detachable linings

Linings protect curtain fabric from the wear and tear caused by bright light and temperature extremes. They also help to exclude the light and provide some extra insulation.

Detachable linings attach to the back of the curtains and have several advantages over a fixed lining. Because linings often wear more quickly than the main curtain fabric and need to be replaced, detachable linings make this job easier. And because they are not an integral part of the curtain, a slight bit of shrinkage will not create a problem in fit.

MATERIALS: Lining fabric (see pages 10 and 11), matching thread, slip-over lining heading tape, curtain track

FABRIC: Follow the instructions for measuring the window and estimate the quantities of fabric as for curtains, allowing a lining width of 1½ to two times the track length for each curtain (see pages 22 and 23). Allow for a hem that ends ¾ inch above the curtain hem edge. Calculate the amount of heading tape that you will need (see pages 22 and 23), allowing extra for positioning.

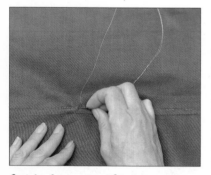

1 Cut out the lining fabric using the established measurements, but allow for each finished lining to be 1 inch narrower than the finished curtain. If it is necessary to piece fabric widths together for a lining, baste and then stitch the widths together with the right sides facing and using flat-fell seams (see page 81).

2 To form the side hems, turn under a double ½-inch hem and press. Stitch close to the inside edge of each hem.

3 Slip the heading tape over the raw top edge of the fabric, with the narrower side of the tape to the right side of the fabric. Pin in place and trim the tape, allowing a 1-inch overlap at each end. At the leading edge (where the curtains will meet), turn under a double ½-inch hem to the wrong side. At the outside edge pull the cords to the top side of the tape, ready for gathering, then turn under a double ½-inch hem to the wrong side. Stitch across the tape ends, stitching through the cords on the leading edge to hold them in place, but leaving those at the outer edge free. Stitch the tape to the curtain top edge.

4 Before you stitch the hem, check the lining length against the curtain. Place the curtain flat and then position the lining over the top of the curtain, matching the top edge to the hook positions. Turn up a double hem ¾ inch shorter than the curtain and stitch. Pull up the cords in the heading tape so that the lining is slightly narrower than the curtain. Hang the detachable lining, fixing the hooks through the lining heading tape first and then through the curtain heading tape. Or, hang the lining from separate rings positioned on tracks below the heading-tape hooks.

A LINING THAT SHOWS

If the lining peeps around the curtain at any position, spoiling the overall effect, cut short lengths of narrow tape and attach one half of a snap fastener to the end. Stitch the opposite end to the inner side hem of the lining and stitch the corresponding snap section to the inside side hem of the curtain. Press snap sections together.

Sheer curtains

Sheer curtains serve a practical purpose, providing privacy and hiding an unattractive view. However, they also can be used for a purely decorative effect.

The curtain shown *at right* is designed to hang from a pole or track, but you can also make sheers with a cased heading and hang them from a curtain wire or rod.

If possible, use wide-width fabric to avoid seaming (seam lines will show up as dark lines against the light). Make the hems as narrow as possible. Also, be sure the fabric is cut square; uneven raw edges will show through the fabric, too. Use a T-square or a right-angle triangle to straighten edges before stitching.

MATERIALS: Sheer fabric, fine thread, desired hanging system, sheer heading tape (if using a curtain track)

FABRIC: To calculate the amount of fabric required, follow the instructions for measuring the window and calculating fabric quantities (see page 22 and 23). Add 8 inches to the length to allow for the hem and heading tape and 1½ inches to the width (for ¾-inch seam allowances). For a curtain that will be hung from a lightweight track, you will need a length of tape the width of the finished curtain plus 4 inches.

CASED HEADING

1 Make sure the fabric edge is square, then cut the number of fabric lengths required to make the full-size curtain. If you are using a patterned fabric, match the pattern design and baste widths together using ladder stitch (see page 78).

2 If you must join widths, use narrow French seams. With wrong sides facing, stitch ⅜ inch from the finished seam-line position. Trim the raw edges to neaten them. Then, with the right sides together, encase these raw edges in a second seam stitched ⅜ inch from the first one (see page 81).

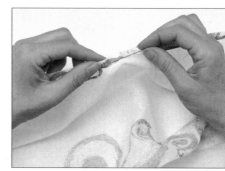

3 To hem the sides, turn in a double ⅜-inch hem down each side and hand-stitch in place.

4 For the lower hem, turn up a double ¾-inch hem and stitch in place.

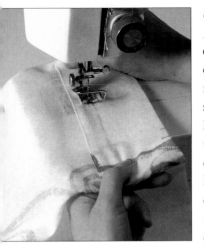

5 To finish the top edge with a casing for a rod, fold over a single, narrow hem along the top edge of the curtain and baste. Fold over again to the desired depth for the ruffle and rod plus ¼ inch. Baste, then machine-stitch close to the hem edge. Measure the casing depth from the stitched hem edge and draw a line across the fabric with tailor's chalk at this depth to divide the ruffle from the casing. Baste, then stitch along this marked line. Slip the rod through the casing. Or use curtain clips as shown at right.

APPLYING HEADING TAPE

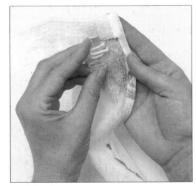

To make a sheer curtain to hang from a lightweight track, turn down a single 1-inch hem along the top edge. Cut the heading tape to the width of the curtain plus 4 inches (for a 2-inch overlap at each end). Position the top tape edge ⅛ inch from the top hem edge, covering the fabric raw edge. Pin and baste in place. On the leading edge, pull the cords to the back of the tape, and knot to secure. Turn in the tape overlap at each end and stitch in place (see steps 5 and 6, page 29). Pull up the gathering cords until the curtain is the correct width; even out the gathers and hang the curtain.

Café curtains

Café curtains screen the lower section of a window while allowing light to pass through the top section. They can be made with a tabbed heading, such as the one shown here, with a scalloped heading (see pages 40 and 41), or with a ruffled heading and a casing through which to pass a stretch wire, pole, or rod (see pages 32 and 33).

Small designs or plain color fabrics are usually best for curtains with a short drop. In addition to cotton and polyester/cotton blends, lighter, semitransparent fabrics such as lace, net, and voile also are suitable. On fine fabrics, line the facing with an interfacing to provide added strength.

MATERIALS: Medium-weight furnishing or sheer fabric, matching thread, pole or rod

FABRIC: Install the hanging system, then measure from its base to the sill and add 2 inches. To work out the curtain width, measure the window from side to side, then add half again or double the measurement. To calculate the amount of fabric required, divide the fabric width into the curtain width measurement, then multiply this number (the number of widths) by the curtain length. Allow extra for matching pattern designs. You also will need enough fabric to make a 4-inch-wide facing to fit the curtain width. For each tab you will need a strip of fabric 8 inches long by twice the chosen tab width plus 1 inch (for ½-inch seam allowances).

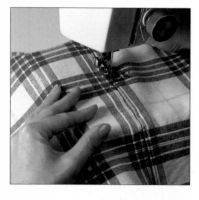

1 Cut out the required fabric lengths to make up the curtain width and stitch together with flat-fell seams (see page 81). Be sure to match the pattern on the joined widths.

2 To hem the sides, turn in a double ½-inch hem down each side of the fabric. Baste in place and then stitch close to the hem edge.

3 Piece facing strips together, if necessary, using flat-fell seams (see page 81). Turn under a double ½-inch hem on one long edge and machine-stitch. Set the facing aside.

On the right side of the curtain, mark tab positions along the top edge, using a fabric pencil. Position the tabs to match the design of the fabric or space them evenly along the curtain width. Place one tab even with each end of the curtain.

4 Cut 8-inch-long strips of fabric for each tab, making each piece twice the required tab width plus 1 inch. Fold each tab in half lengthwise with the right sides facing. Stitch together along the long raw edge, using a ½-inch seam allowance. Press the seam open. Turn the tab right side out and press with the seam in the center back.

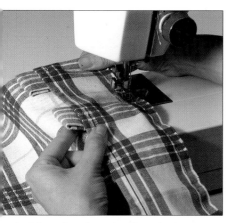

TAB KITS

Tab kits, which contain iron-on buckram cut to size, require no sewing. Simply follow the instructions provided to attach the buckram to your chosen tab fabric. The kits also contain self-cover buttons and butterfly clips to fix the heading in place.

5 Fold each tab in half with the seam on the inside. Align the tabs with the pencil marks on the curtain edge, right sides facing and raw edges aligned. Pin the tabs in place. With raw edges even and right sides facing, place the curtain facing over the top edge of the curtain (tabs in between). Pin, baste, then stitch the facing and curtain together across the top, using ½-inch seam allowance and starting and stopping 1 inch from each end.

6 Turn the facing to the wrong side of the curtain. Turn in the facing side hems and slip-stitch them to the curtain. Hang the curtain and pin up the bottom hem. Remove the curtain to stitch and press the hem, then rehang the curtain.

Lined curtains

Lined curtains hang better than unlined curtains. The lining also helps to block the light, provides some insulation, and protects the curtain fabric from sunlight damage.

The simplest way to make lined curtains (and the method used for this project) is to stitch the lining and top fabric together along the sides and top and then take up the hems separately. The lining piece is cut narrower than the curtain width, so that when the curtain is turned right side out, the seams joining the two pieces are hidden on the wrong side of the curtain.

MATERIALS: Furnishing fabric, lining fabric, matching sewing thread, deep triple-pleat heading tape, track or pole

FABRIC: To calculate the amount of curtain fabric required, follow the instructions for measuring the window an calculating fabric quantities on pages 22 and 23. You will need lining fabric to the finished curtain size. Use measurement W (see pages 22 and 23) to work out the amount of heading tape needed.

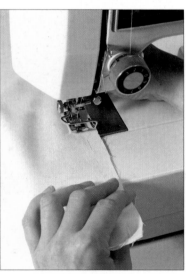

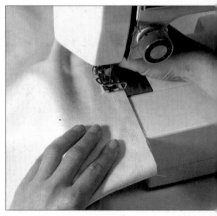

1 Cut the required lengths of fabric, allowing for pattern repeats, then pin and baste the widths together. To join widths of patterned fabric, work from the right side and use a ladder stitch (see page 78). Turn to the wrong side and stitch the widths together using a ½-inch seam allowance. Press the seams open.

2 Cut the lengths of lining fabric 3 inches shorter than the curtain length. With the right sides facing, pin and baste the lining widths together, then stitch, using a ½-inch seam allowance. Press the seams open. Trim away 2 inches from each side edge of the lining.

3 Mark the center on the top and bottom edges of the fabric and th lining. With right sides together, place the lining atop the curtain, matching them at one side edge. Offset the lining top edge from the fabric top edge by the width of the curtain tape (the center marks will not align). Pin, baste, and stitch the side edge, using a ½-inch seam allowance. Start at the top and stop 4 inches from the bottom edge. Repea for the opposite side edge.

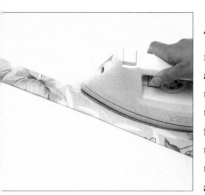

4 Turn the curtain right side out and match up the centers on the lining and fabric. Baste the fabrics together along the top ge of the lining and pin together along the ttom edge. Press well to form the curtain side ges and then remove the pins. Because the ning is narrower than the curtain fabric, there ll be a 2-inch overlap of the curtain fabric on ch side of the lining.

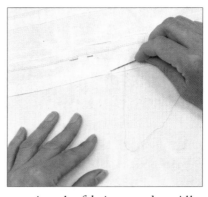

5 Fold over the top edge of the curtain fabric to the wrong side so it just covers the lining's raw edge; pin it in place. Position the heading tape just below the top edge, covering the fabric raw edge. Allow a 2-inch overlap of tape at each end. Position the tape pleats to allow for a flat area on the leading edge of one panel and a pleat on the other panel; that way, the pleats will appear equally spaced across the curtains when they are drawn. Baste and stitch the tape in place (see steps 5 and 6, page 29).

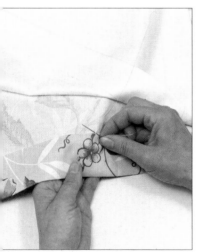

6 Before hemming the curtain, pull up the cords d hang the curtains to check e length. Pin up double hems both the top fabric and the ning fabric. The finished edge the lining hem should lie 1⅝ ches above the curtain hem d the finished curtain hem ould be 2 inches wide. Trim brics if necessary, miter rners (see pages 82 and 83), d stitch lining and top fabric ms separately.

Interlined curtains

Interlined curtains have a layer of fabric sandwiched between the main fabric and the lining. This adds extra insulation and provides a sumptuous look and feel to the curtains.

The main fabric and interlining are first lockstitched together to act as one layer, and then the lining is lockstitched to this. Lead-weight tape is included in the hem so the curtains will hang well. A deep goblet heading completes the rich effect of these elegant curtains.

MATERIALS: Medium-weight to heavyweight furnishing fabric, lining fabric, interlining, matching thread, goblet-pleat heading tape, lead-weight tape, track or pole

FABRIC: Follow the instructions for measuring the window and calculating the fabric quantities (see pages 22 and 23), allowing 4 inches for the hem plus the width of the chosen heading tape for the top edge. Allow extra for matching the fabric pattern. You will need the same amount of interlining as the main curtain fabric and enough lining fabric to fit the finished curtain size. Use measurement W (see pages 22 and 23) to give you the required amount of heading tape. The length of the lead-weight tape should equal the length of the finished curtain hems.

1 Cut out the lengths of the main fabric and interlining, using the measurements that you have calculated. Cut the lining to the finished curtain size. Join widths of main fabric and lining as needed (see steps 1 and 2, page 36).

2 To join widths of interlining, place two lengths side by side on a large flat surface, overlapping the joining edges by about ½ inch. Use a herringbone stitch (see page 79) to join the widths together. Continue joining interlining widths in this manner until you have enough to make up the curtain size.

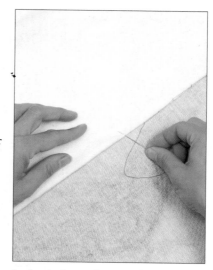

3 Lay the interlining out flat and place the main fabric, right side up, on top. Pin the two materials together from the top to the bottom down the center. Fold back the fabric to this center pinned line and lockstitch to the interlining down the center (see page 78). Smooth the fabric back over the interlining for 15 inches and lockstitch together again in a line parallel to the first. Continue in this manner until you reach the curtain edge. Baste the two materials together down the side. Repeat in the same manner from the center to the opposite side.

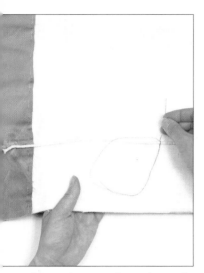

4 Fold a single 2-inch hem to the wrong side on each side. Turn up a 4-inch single hem along the lower edge and press in place. Open out the hem, lay the length of lead-weight tape along the pressed hem line, and stitch in place at evenly spaced intervals. Miter the hem corners (see page 83) and slip-stitch the angled miter seam. Work herringbone stitches along all the raw hem edges.

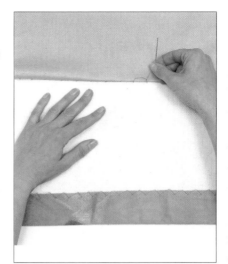

5 Place the lining over the interlined main fabric with wrong sides facing. Pin down the center and lockstitch the lining to the interlining as in Step 3; finish each line of stitching just above the hem edge. Leave the side edges unstitched. Trim the lining fabric at the edges, if necessary, so that the raw edges are flush with the finished main curtain edges.

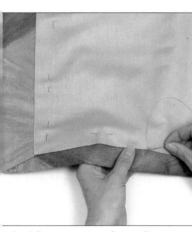

6 Turn under a single 2-inch hem along the lower lining edge and a 1-inch hem down each side; press in place. Create a mock miter in the lining hem corners (see page 82). Press the lining hem edges and slip-stitch the lining to the curtain fabric at the sides and along the lower hem.

7 Before adding the heading tape, check the length of the curtains. Then turn in the top edge and attach the heading tape (see pages 28 and 29). Pull up the cords in the heading tape and attach a covered button to each pleat point. Secure the cords on a cord tidy and hang the curtains.

Scalloped headings

Scalloped headings create a decorative top edge and are suitable for unlined or lightweight lined curtains. The size of the scallop depends on the length of the curtain. For full-length curtains, allow a scallop width of 5 to 6 inches and a depth equal to half the width measurement. On a short curtain, scallops will look better if they are smaller.

   This curtain is hung from fabric ties sewn in place between the main curtain fabric and the facing. Use ribbon instead of fabric for the ties, if you wish.

MATERIALS: Medium-weight furnishing fabric or sheer fabric, medium-weight iron-on interfacing, matching thread, pole or rod, posterboard for pattern template

FABRIC: Install the hanging system and measure from its base to the sill or floor for the curtain length. Allow 1½ times the pole length for the fabric width. Follow the instructions on pages 22 and 23 for calculating fabric quantities. For full-length curtains, cut a strip for the top facing 5 inches wide by the width of the curtain. Cut the interfacing 4 inches wide by the width of the curtain. For each tie, cut a strip of fabric 30 inches long and twice the finished width plus 1 inch (for ½-inch seam allowances).

1 Cut out and make up the curtain width (see steps 1 and 2, page 28). Iron the length of interfacing to the wrong side at the top of the curtain, matching it to the top and side edges. Turn under and stitch single 1-inch side hems, leaving the top 5 inches unstitched.

2 Turn under a single ½-inch hem along the bottom edge of the facing and stitch. With right sides together and raw edges matching, pin the facing to the top edge of the curtain. Stitch down the side edges. Baste along the top edge only; do not stitch.

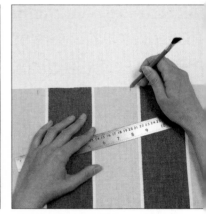

3 Mark the scallop positions on the top edge of the fabric. The scallops and the spaces in between (which should be slightly wider than the width of the fabric ties) need to work out equally across the width of the curtain, with a space for a tie at each end. Center a scallop in the center of the curtain.

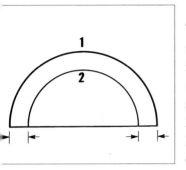

4 Make a pattern template for each of the scallop shapes. Mark one half-circle (1) onto osterboard, using a saucer or compass. This the stitching line. Mark a second half-circle inch inside the first (2). This is the cutting ne. Cut out the shapes.

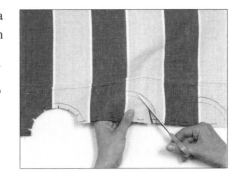

5 Line up the larger template (1) with each marked position for a scallop shape and trace it onto the fabric. Position the smaller template (2) centered inside the marked scallop shape, lining up the straight edge with the curtain edge. Trace the shape. Baste, then stitch each scallop separately. Cut out the scallops, following the cutting line, then cut notches into the curved seam allowance.

6 Fold each tie strip in half lengthwise with right sides facing. Stitch down the long edge and across one short edge. Turn right side out. Turn in the raw short edge and slip-stitch the opening closed. Fold the ties in half and place them etween the main fabric and facing, keeping the fold flush ith the curtain's top edge. Stitch across each top edge ½ inch om the raw edge. Press, turn right side out, and press again. lip-stitch the lower facing edge to the main curtain fabric.

7 To finish the curtain, tie the fabric ties over the rod and turn up the lower hem. Remove the curtain to stitch the hem, then rehang the curtain.

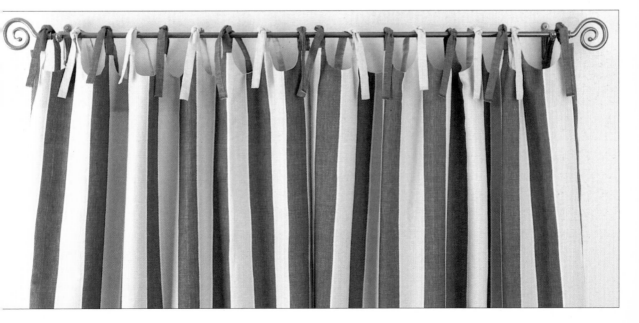

Curtain Dressing

The addition of a gathered or shaped valance or even a simple tieback can make an ordinary window treatment more sophisticated.

Tiebacks serve a practical purpose, holding curtains away from the window when they are drawn back. They also create an additional decorative element and can be made in both classic and contemporary styles.

A valance, draped heading, and traditionally arranged swag and tails are positioned above a pair of curtains or a blind to hide the top of the treatment and create a neater overall finish.

This chapter contains

Classic tiebacks	44
Creative tiebacks	46
Simple valances	48
Shaped valances	50
Draped headings	52
Swag and tails	54

Classic tiebacks

A stiffened, shaped tieback—one that widens toward the center and curves to follow the curtain's gathers—is the classic way to hold back curtains.

Tiebacks may be positioned one-third of the way down from the top of the curtain, halfway down the curtain, or one-third up from its lower edge, depending on the shape of the window.

MATERIALS: Furnishing fabric or fabric and lining, matching thread, iron-on interfacing, paper for making the pattern, cord (for the cord-trimmed tieback only), self-cover button (for the scallop-edge tieback only), rings and hooks for attaching

FABRIC: Measure the curtain for the tieback length required. Enlarge the pattern (see pages 90 and 91). For each tieback, you will need two pieces of fabric this size (or one of fabric and one of lining) plus a ½-inch seam allowance, and one piece of interfacing the size of each finished tieback. For the cord-trimmed tieback, measure along the outside edge of the pattern (the finished edge) and add 2 inches for the length of cord you will need.

CORD-TRIMMED TIEBACK

1 Decide where to place the tieback, trying different positions with a length of string or fabric. Mark the wall where the hook will go, using a pencil. Hold a tape measure around the curtain from this marked point to determine the finished tieback length. Screw the hooks into the wall.

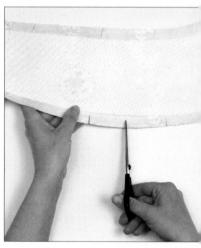

3 Center the interfacing piece on the wrong side of the front tieback shape and iron in place, following the manufacturer's instructions. When the interfacing is affixed, clip into the seam allowance, then press the fabric allowance to the wrong side of the tieback, covering the edge of the interfacing. Baste in place.

2 Enlarge Pattern A on page 90. Place the fold edge on folded paper and cut out a full-size pattern. Use the pattern to cut out the tieback interfacing. Then, for each tieback, cut two shapes from the fabric (the pattern includes a ½ inch seam allowance).

4 Press the seam allowance on the lining to the wrong side, clipping into the seam allowance to make it lie flat. Place the lining and the interfaced tieback together with the wrong sides facing and matching raw edges. Slip-stitch the pieces together, leaving a 1-inch gap in one end of the tieback. Slip the end of the cord into the gap, then slip-stitch the rest of the cord around the edge of the tieback. Tuck the opposite cord end into the gap, stitch the cord ends together, and slip-stitch the opening closed. Attach a ring to each end of the tieback and hang.

SCALLOP-EDGE TIEBACK

1 Work out the tieback size and cut out a pattern (see steps 1 and 2, Cord-Trimmed Tieback) using Pattern B on page 91.

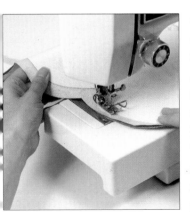

2 Cut out the interfacing, main fabric, and lining. Attach interfacing to the wrong side of the main fabric (see Step 3, Cord-Trimmed Tieback). With right sides facing, place the lining over the main fabric. Stitch ½ inch from the raw edges along the scalloped edge. Trim the seam allowance around the inner points and curves. Turn right side out and press. Turn in the raw edges and slip-stitch the opening closed. Make a self-cover button and stitch it to the tieback. Stitch a ring to each end of the tieback and hang.

Creative tiebacks

A quick and easy way to create your own decorative tiebacks is to use curtain heading tape. Use gathered heading tape and fabric to match the curtain. Or choose from smocked, lattice, and trellis tapes to create an even more ornate finish.

For a three-dimensional look, make twisted tiebacks from padded fabric tubes that complement the curtains.

MATERIALS:

Gathered tieback: Furnishing fabric, lattice heading tape, matching thread, dressmaker's pencil, rings and tieback hooks
Twisted tieback: Two contrasting or complementary furnishing fabrics, batting, matching thread, rings and tieback hooks

FABRIC:

Gathered tieback: Measure the tieback length required (see Step 1, pages 44 and 45). For each tieback, cut two pieces of fabric 2½ times this length by a width equal to the width of the heading tape plus 1 inch (for ½-inch seam allowances). For the heading tape, cut a strip the finished length of the tieback, plus 5 inches for positioning.
Twisted tieback: For each tieback, cut a 4-inch-wide fabric strip 2¼ times the finished length, plus 1 inch (for ½-inch seam allowances). Cut two 3-inch-wide strips of batting 2¼ times the finished length.

GATHERED TIEBACK

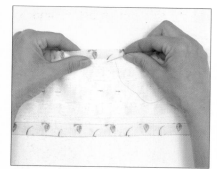

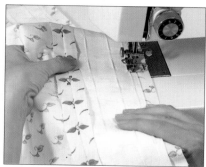

1 Cut and piece fabric to the required length for each tieback. Press seams open. Pin the two tieback pieces together with the right sides facing and raw edges matching. Center the heading tape on the wrong side of one tieback piece and pin it in place. Secure the cords at one end of the tape; pull them free at the other end. Trim the tape to fit. Baste all three sections together along one long edge only.

2 Stitch along the basted edge close to the edge of the heading tape. Open out the joined lengths and press the seam open. Stitch the tape in place along the other long edge, attaching it to one tieback piece only. Press this seam allowance over the edge of the heading tape. On the other long edge, press under a ½-inch hem to the wrong side. Match finished long edges and slip-stitch closed.

3 Turn in the fabric at the end of the tape where the cords are tied and slip-stitch the opening closed. With the dressmaker's pencil, draw a line ¾ inch from each long edge. Machine-stitch along these lines. This gives the tieback a neat finish. Pull the tape cords to gather the tieback to the finished length. Turn in the raw end and slip-stitch the opening closed. Attach a curtain ring to each end of the tieback.

WISTED TIEBACK

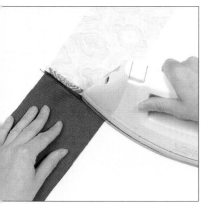

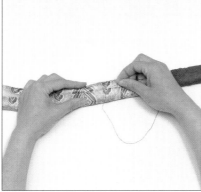

1 Cut out one strip from each of the two fabrics. To join he strips, place one strip on op of the other with the right ides facing and raw edges natching. Stitch across one hort end ½ inch from the raw dge. Press the seam open. You ow have one 4-inch-wide, louble-length strip of the two lifferent fabrics.

2 To make the tube, place the strip right side down. Turn in and press ⅝ inch along one long edge. Center the batting on top. Bring both long edges of the fabric to the center, pinning the folded edge over the raw edge and forming a tube around the batting. Slip-stitch along the pinned edge to hold it in place. Trim the batting at each end. Turn in the raw edge and baste closed.

3 Fold the tube in half crosswise at the join and stitch across ½ inch from the fold. Turn down each corner on the fold diagonally to the back side, forming a point. Stitch to secure, and attach a curtain ring. Evenly twist the two lengths, keeping the seam at the back. Pin the ends together. Check the length, then form a point at this end, as before, and attach a ring.

Simple valances

A simple valance has a gathered or pleated heading and is constructed like a curtain. It can be embellished in a number of ways, including a bound edge, a ruffle, a border of contrasting fabric, and a fringe. A valance can be paired with blinds or used to hide an unattractive curtain top or track. Either way, it completes the decorative effect of a window treatment.

MATERIALS: *Gathered valance:* Furnishing fabric and lining, fabric for border, matching thread, heading tape, valance rail *Pleated valance:* Furnishing fabric and lining, matching thread, heading tape, valance rail

FABRIC: See pages 22 and 23 for calculating fabric and heading tape quantities. The valance length should be about one-sixth the curtain length. Add 4 inches to the heading tape measurement. *For a gathered valance:* For fabric width, allow 2½ times the finished valance width. For the border, make a strip 5 inches wide by the fabric width. *For a pleated valance:* For fabric width, allow three times the finished valance width

GATHERED VALANCE

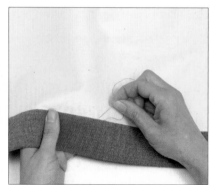

1 To join plain fabric widths, cut and piece the widths of fabric to obtain the valance length, using ½-inch seam allowances. Press the seams open. On patterned fabric, baste together from the right side using a ladder stitch (see page 78). Cut each lining length 6 inches shorter than the top fabric. With right sides facing, join widths as for the valance fabric. Trim ½ inch off each lining (short) side edge.

2 Place the lining and fabric with right sides facing, matching one side edge and the bottom edge. Stitch the side seam. Repeat for the other side seam. Turn right side out, centering the lining, and press. Baste together along the lining top edge. Align the border with the bottom valance edge, right sides facing and ½ inch of the border overlapping at each short end; stitch. Turn in ½ inch on the remaining three raw edges of the border. Fold border to the back of the valance and slip-stitch in place.

3 To attach the heading tape, fold over the top edge of the fabric to the wrong side of the valance, just covering the top edge of the lining. Press in place, then place the tape over this single hem just below the top edge and covering the fabric raw edge. Allow a 2-inch overlap of tape at each end and baste to hold. Stitch the heading tape in place (see Step 5, page 29). Draw up the gathers, arranging them evenly and fit to the valance rail.

PLEATED VALANCE

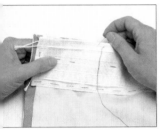

1 Cut out the fabric and the lining and join to obtain the desired width, following steps 1 and 2 of Gathered Valance (omitting the border). Turn up the hem. Baste the pleated heading tape in position, allowing a 2-inch overlap of tape at each end. Baste to hold. Then stitch the heading tape in place (see Step 5, page 29).

2 To draw up the pleats, take the cords at the end of the heading tape and pull them through. The pleats will be drawn into place as the cords are pulled, and the top cord will hold the pleats in place. When all the pleats are drawn up, knot the cord ends to secure. Check to make sure the pleats are even, then press the pleats in position for a crisp finish. Fit the valance to the rail with curtain hooks.

Shaped valances

Shaped valances, also called pelmets, combine the rigidity and structure of a cornice with the fabric of a valance. The stiffened fabric attaches to a shelf above the curtain track to give an ornate finish to a window treatment.

Shaped valances are often made by stapling fabric over a padded board. The one shown here uses a heavy self-adhesive paper called a pelmet former. If you can't find this product in your area, you can achieve a similar effect by cutting the valance shape from foam-core board and gluing fabric over it.

Before making the valance, attach a shelf to the wall as you would a furring strip (see page 61). Make the shelf from a 1×4 cut 2 inches longer than the curtain track. Position the shelf 2 inches above the curtain, and secure it with L-shape brackets at 8-inch intervals.

MATERIALS: Medium-weight furnishing fabric, lining fabric, 24-inch-wide double-sided self-adhesive pelmet former, matching thread, valance shelf, hook-and-loop fastening tape, dressmaker's pencil

FABRIC: To calculate the total width of fabric required, attach the valance shelf (see page 61), then measure around the shelf, adding the front and both side measurements together; add 2 inches to this measurement for the valance width. Make the valance pattern (see Step 1, below), then measure its depth and add 2 inches. Calculate the number of fabric widths needed, dividing the total width required by the fabric width measurement; then multiply this by the valance depth measurement. You will need fabric and lining this size, self-adhesive pelmet former to the valance depth by the total fabric width, and fastening tape equal to the total fabric width.

1 To create a shaped edge, use a design on the back of the pelmet former or use the grid on the backing paper to make your own. (The zigzag edge shown here measures 8 inches deep and 7¼ inches wide.) Measure the length of the valance shelf, including the sides. Mark vertical lines on the grid at each corner where the front of the valance meets the sides and one at the center front of the valance.

2 Join fabric widths if required, positioning a full width of fabric in the center and partial widths at the outside edges. Press the fabric, then mark the center point on the wrong side. Center the pattern on the wrong side of the fabric, matching center marks, and draw around it with the dressmaker's pencil. Mark a second line 1 inch outside the first and cut out the fabric following this line. Use the fabric as a pattern for cutting out a piece of lining fabric.

3 Lift the backing paper at the center slightly, then cut ertically through the paper only. his allows you to adhere one-half [the pelmet former at a time. /orking from the center, peel ack a small area of the backing aper and smooth the pelmet rmer over the wrong side of the bric. Continue in this manner to e outer edge. Repeat to adhere e other half.

4 Clip or notch into the seam allowance on corners and at curves. Peel off the top paper on the pelmet former and fold and smooth the seam allowances onto the tacky surface. On the lining piece, press under a 1-inch hem, then gently smooth the lining, right side up, in place over the pelmet former. Slip-stitch the lining to the fabric around the edges to hold them in place.

5 To install the valance, separate the hook-and-loop fastening tape. Attach the hook strip to the edge of the shelf. Then press the loop strip along the top back edge of the shaped valance. Crease the valance to fit around the shelf corners, then press the hook and loop strips together to hold the valance in place.

Draped headings

A length of single-width fabric, draped over a curtain pole or metal holdbacks, balances well with the simple lines of a Roman blind or roller blind. It also can be used on its own to make a decorative frame for a window or doorway.

The two examples of a draped heading shown here can be made in the minimum of time and require almost no sewing.

MATERIALS:

Draped curtain pole: Lightweight furnishing fabric, matching thread, pole and hardware, curtain clips
Archway drape: Sheer fabric, matching thread, three metal holdbacks and hardware

FABRIC:

Draped curtain pole: Choose a fabric without a one-way design. Fix the pole in place, then use string to measure the length of the fabric, adding 1 inch all around for hems.
Archway drape: Choose a fabric without a one-way design. Fix holdbacks (see Step 1 at right). Use string to check the drape depth and length. Add 1 inch all around for hems.

DRAPED CURTAIN POLE

1 Fix the pole in place (see page 21). Depending on how much of the window top you want the swags to cover, position the pole between 4 and 8 inches above the window's frame.

2 Cut the selvages from the fabric. Turn under a ½-inch double hem to the wrong side on all raw edges and stitch. To create wedge-shape tails, cut the fabric ends on the bias before hemming.

3 To create even-length tails, loop the fabric over the pole, starting at the center of the pole and the center of the fabric. Secure with curtain clips. Loosely arrange swirls of fabric toward each pole end, making sure the tails are the same length before securing. Arrange fabric to cover the clips.

ARCHWAY DRAPE

1 Begin by fixing the metal holdbacks to the wall. Place the center holdback above the door or window and the side holdbacks the same distance out to each side—about 3 to 5 inches, depending on the width of the fabric.

2 Cut the selvages from the fabric, then turn in ½-inch double hems to the wrong side on all raw edges and stitch to secure. (Hand-stitching will be less obvious on sheer fabrics than machine-stitching.)

3 Fold the fabric in half crosswise to find the center. Loop the fabric center around the top holdback, keeping the right side of the fabric to the front. Arrange fabric in a swag to each side and secure by looping fabric around the side holdbacks.

Swag and tails

This classic swag-and-tails design consists of four pieces: a pleated front swag, two pleated tails for the sides, and a long, thin rectangle that covers the top of the shelf. The swag and tails are stitched to the rectangle shape, creating a single unit. While you may find stapling the individual sections to the shelf preferable to stitching them together, the stitched assembly has its advantages. It keeps the pleats permanently intact and allows for the curtain's easy removal and return to the valance shelf when laundering is necessary.

MATERIALS: Old sheets for the pattern, furnishing fabric, lining, air-soluble marker, matching thread, 1×4 valance shelf, staple gun or hammer and tacks

FABRIC: Attach the shelf as for a Roman blind (page 61). Cut a covering the size of the top of the shelf, adding a ¾-inch seam allowance on all sides. Measure patterns (see below) for fabric and lining quantities, adding a ¾-inch seam allowance on all sides. Allow extra for pattern matching.

1 Cut the valance shelf covering from fabric as directed above. Mark the centers and corner points on all sides directly on the seam line. For the swag pattern, staple an old sheet to the top of the shelf as follows: Arrange the swag to the chosen depth in the center front and secure with staples; pleat the fabric at each end, pinning the pleats in place. With an air-soluble marker, draw a line across the top edge (even with the shelf). Also mark the center point and the pleats. Cut off the excess sheet.

2 Measure the desired tail length. (The length is usually one-third to two-thirds the curtain length.) Cut two pieces of sheet to this length, cutting the lower edge on the bias to form a narrowing tail. With the longer edge to the outside, staple one tail around the corner of the valance shelf. Arrange the pleats, then pin and mark their positions on the top and lower edges. Repeat to make a mirror image on the other corner.

3 To create the top swag, cut fabric and lining pieces, following your pattern and adding ¾-inch seam allowance on all sides. (The pleat folds will show as zigzag edges.) Place fabric and lining with right sides together and stitch along the front curved edge only. Turn right side out and press. Baste across the zigzag edge. Press the marked pleats and baste in place. Check the effect and then stitch across the pleated seam line. Locate and mark the center on the pleated edge of the swag.

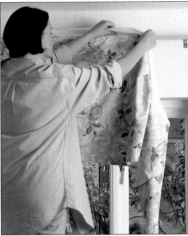

4 From the main fabric and lining, cut out the tails, adding ¾-inch seam allowances all around. For each tail, place lining and fabric pieces together with the right sides facing. Stitch along the sides and the lower edge. Clip the corners, turn right side out, and press. Fold the pleats on each tail as marked on the pattern piece, then baste across the pleats on the seam line.

5 With right sides facing and matching the center points, pin the top edge of the swag to the front edge of the valance covering. Baste in place. Pin and baste the tails around each corner in the same way. Place the curtain dressing over the valance shelf; check the effect and adjust, if necessary. Remove the curtain dressing, then stitch the pieces together using a ¾-inch seam allowance. Trim the seam allowance and clip the corners. Press and rehang.

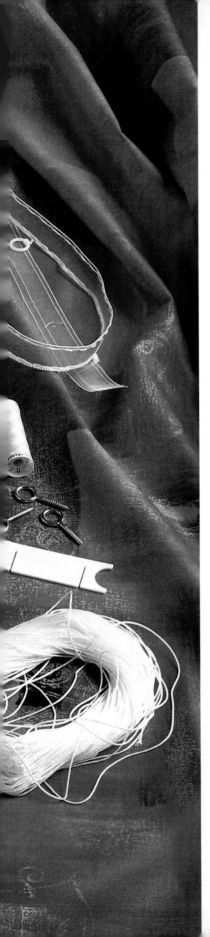

Before You Begin: Blinds

A versatile alternative to curtains, blinds can be raised during the day or, when made from finer fabrics, left down to provide privacy.

Though the amount of fabric required depends on the style of blind chosen, the simpler styles use far less fabric than curtains. However, they do not provide the same amount of insulation. If you need window treatments to provide extra insulation, consider using both a blind and a curtain on the same window.

This chapter introduces the principal types of blinds, shows how to put up an appropriate hanging system, and gives all the information needed to measure accurately and calculate the quantities of fabric and materials required.

This chapter contains

Blind styles	58
Hanging blinds	60
Calculating quantities	62

Blind styles

Different blinds suit different situations and types of fabric. Here are some tips on how they work, areas or windows for which they are especially suited, fabrics to choose, and final finishing touches you can apply.

ROLLER BLIND

◀ A roller blind is the simplest form of blind. It uses a minimum amount of fabric and rolls up into a narrow strip at the top of the window, allowing the maximum amount of light into a room. Roller blinds are a practical choice for kitchen and bathroom windows or for use at a window with a beautiful view. The simple shape of the blind also lends itself to the addition of a decoratively shaped edge.

ROMAN BLIND

◀ A Roman blind lies flat to the window in the same way as a roller blind. However, cords threaded through rings on tapes at the back of the blind create neat horizontal pleats when it is pulled up. This type of blind is suitable for use in most rooms and can be made from closely woven medium-weight, fabrics or from sheer fabrics. Borders at the sides and lower edge give a sophisticated finish and are a good way to add width if the fabric is narrower than the window. Roman blinds also look effective when teamed with curtains made in a complementary fabric.

ESTOON BLIND

◄ The ultimate in romance, a festoon blind is gathered both horizontally and vertically. This type of blind is often used to give privacy during the day or provide some shade in a sunny room. It's most often made from sheer fabrics or finer fabrics such as a polyester/cotton blend. The ruched effect of a festoon blind looks best outlined with a ruffle.

AUSTRIAN BLIND

◄ An Austrian blind, which hangs in curtainlike gathers and falls in deep swags at the lower edge, creates a grand effect ideally suited to living rooms and bedrooms. Austrian blinds can be lined or unlined. For a decorative finish, trim the lower edge with fringes or ruffles.

Hanging blinds

Blinds are fixed in place in a number of different ways, depending on the type of blind and the installation system you decide to use.

ROLLER BLIND

Roller blinds are the simplest type of blind to fit. The kit includes brackets, which must be attached to each side of the window to hold the roller. The blind is attached to the roller and fitted back into the brackets.

1 Buy a blind kit to fit the space. Attach the blind brackets to the wall, checking the manufacturer's instructions to make sure the left and right brackets are correctly placed. Allow 1 to 1⅜ inches above the brackets for the thickness of fabric around the pole. Mark the positions for the screws square with the window, and fix the brackets in place (see pages 20 and 21).

2 Measure the distance between the brackets and check this measurement against the length of the roller. If necessary, cut the roller to size by sawing off the bare timber end. Place the cap over the sawn end and gently hammer the pin in place through the center. Check the roller fit by placing it in the brackets.

OMAN BLIND

oman blinds are attached to a furring strip or 1×1 fixed above a window. Screw eyes are positioned ong the underside of the strip to align with the vertical tapes on the blind. They are used to take the ngths of cord to one side of the window so the blind can be raised and lowered easily.

2 Position the brackets about 1⅛ inches from each end of the furring strip, flush with the back edge. Mark the position of the screw holes and screw the brackets to the furring strip. Holding the strip with the attached brackets against the placement marks on the wall, mark the position of the screw holes for the brackets on

Decide where to position the blind and lightly mark the placement on the wall or window frame ith a pencil. Measure this distance, then cut the rring strip to this length. Sand the ends and check e fit. If the blind is to fit in a recessed window, the rip should just slip neatly into the space.

the wall or woodwork. (Use a level to make sure the wood strip is horizontal.) Take the furring strip down and remove the screws securing it to the brackets (you will reattach it later). Attach the brackets at the marked positions (see pages 20 and 21). Once in place, the brackets can be painted to match the wall.

STOON AND AUSTRIAN BLINDS

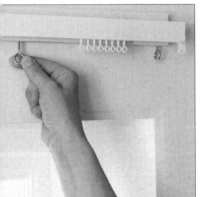

The simplest method of fixing a festoon or Austrian blind is to use the special blind track that comes with integral cord holders (see pages 12

d 13). This type of track is installed in the same ay as ordinary curtain track. You also can put up a rring strip with a simple curtain track mounted on e front of it. Screw eyes affixed to the underside ke the cords out to the side (see above).

Measure the distance the furring strip is to cover and cut it to fit. Attach the brackets as for a Roman blind. Cut a length of curtain track to fit the front of the furring strip.

Screw the track brackets to the wood, then fit the track with the curtain hooks and an end-stop at each end. Once the blind is complete, fix screw eyes along the lower edge of the furring strip, aligning them with the vertical curtain tapes.

Calculating quantities

Most blinds are made to fit within a window recess or, if the window is flush with the wall, to cover the window. Blinds for flush windows usually are made slightly larger than the window to prevent light appearing around the blind edges. However, they also can be made significantly wider or longer than the window, if desired.

MEASURING UP
Recessed window

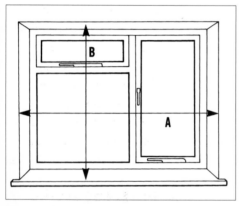

To fit into a recess, the blind should be ½ inch smaller than the recess on each side. You'll cut the fabric for the blind so it's slightly narrower than the furring strip to which you attach the blind's hardware. First measure the recess width and subtract ¾ inch. This is measurement A. Then measure from the top of the recess to the window sill and subtract ½ inch. This is measurement B.

Flush window

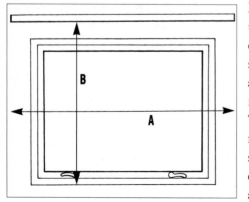

Measure the width of the window from the outer edge on each side of the frame and add 4 inches. This is measurement A. Then measure from the hanging system to the lower edge of the frame and add 4 inches. This is measurement B. If you prefer to make a blind that sits above the window sill, omit the extra 4 inches.

FABRIC AND MATERIAL REQUIREMENT
Festoon blind

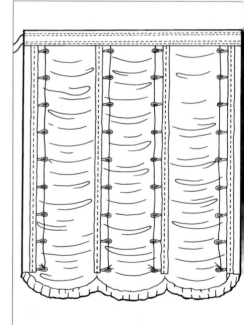

Fabric: Twice measurement A for the width; 1½ times measurement B for the length. *Heading tape:* Twice measurement A, plus 4 inches. *Festoon blind tape:* The number of vertical tapes times the fabric length. *Cord:* Twice measurement B plus measurement A, times the number of vertical tapes. *Blind track:* Measurement A. *Rings:* One for each vertical tape.

oman blind

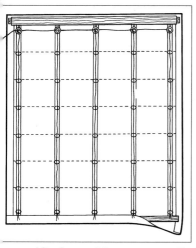

Fabric: Measurement A plus 3 inches for the width; measurement B plus 5 inches for the length. *Lining:* Measurement A for the width; measurement B minus 2 inches for the length.

oman blind tape: Measurement B times the number f vertical tapes. *Cord:* Twice measurement B plus easurement A, times the number of vertical tapes. *ook-and-loop fastening tape:* Measurement A. *Furring rip:* One ¾×1¾-inch by measurement A. *L-shape ackets:* Two 1¾×1¾-inch brackets. Use more rackets for strips longer than 4 feet. *Lath:* One ×1-inch by measurement A. *Rings:* One for each rtical tape. *Screw eyes:* One for each vertical tape.

Austrian blind

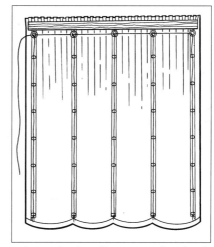

Fabric: Two to 2½ times measurement A for the width; measurement B plus 16 to 20 inches for the length. *Lining:* The fabric width minus 2 inches for the width; the fabric length minus the heading tape depth plus 1 inch for the length. *Blind track:* Measurement A. *Heading tape:* Fabric width plus 4 inches. *Austrian blind tape:* Fabric length times the number of vertical tapes. *Cord:* Twice measurement B plus measurement A, times the number of vertical tapes. *Rings:* One for each vertical tape. If using rings only, plan on one for each vertical pleat on each drawn horizontal line it crosses plus the edges (see pages 72 and 73).

oller blind

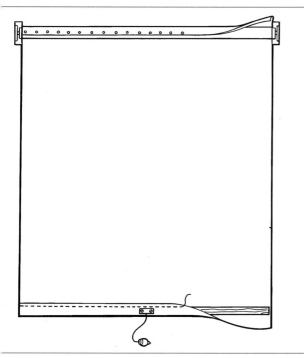

Fabric: The width of the roller plus 2 inches for the width; measurement B plus 12 inches for the length. Allow extra for a shaped edge. *Roller blind kit:* Measurement A or the next size up, if not available.

JOINING FABRIC WIDTHS

For blinds that need more than one length of fabric to make up the width, simply multiply the measurement for the length by the number of widths to find the amount of fabric required.

If you choose a fabric with a design that needs to be matched across the width, you will need to allow for extra fabric. The retailer will check the pattern repeat and help you calculate the amount of extra fabric required. A bold motif looks best when it is centered on a blind, so allow for this, too.

Making Blinds

This chapter gives step-by-step instructions on how to make a variety of blinds, from a simple roller blind, to a romantic festoon, to the more elaborate Austrian and Roman blinds.

Soft blinds are made from a rectangle of fabric that is prepared in much the same way as a curtain and can be lined or unlined. Austrian, Roman, and festoon blinds have vertical tapes positioned on the reverse side, and it is the way these blinds are gathered that creates the different effects.

Blinds are the ideal treatment for a window where you want to introduce the maximum amount of light or enjoy the view. Most blinds use less fabric than curtains, but they also provide less insulation. The ultimate window treatment is to combine curtains and blinds for a decorative and practical solution.

This chapter contains

Roller blind	66
Roman blind	68
Festoon blind	70
Austrian blind	72

Roller blind

Roller blinds look best when made from a fabric with a bold design and finished with a decorative edge.

If possible, choose prestiffened fabric, because it comes in a range of widths and can be wiped clean. (Joined widths of fabric aren't satisfactory for roller blinds.) Or use a closely woven cotton that's been treated with fabric stiffener.

Begin by attaching brackets to the top of the window and cutting the roller to fit the space (see pages 60 and 61).

MATERIALS: Prestiffened blind fabric closely woven cotton fabric treated with fabric stiffener, matching threac roller blind kit, cord holder, double-sided self-adhesive tape, staples anc a staple gun or tacks and a hammer

FABRIC: Follow the instructions for measuring the window and calculatir the quantities of fabric and materials required (see pages 62 and 63).

1 Lay the fabric out flat. Mark the cutting lines with a dressmaker's pencil, centering the design. Make sure the corners form perfect right angles (see pages 24 and 25), then cut out.

2 On woven cotton, neaten the sides and top edge with a zigzag stitch (hems will stop the blind from rolling up smoothly). This is necessary for prestiffened fabric

3 Cut a decorative edge, following the fabric's design. Form a channel at the back of the blind above the shaped edge, wide enough to take the lath, and machine stitch in place. Slip the lath into the casing and stitch across the ends to close. On the wrong side of the blind, mark the center point on the lath. Attach the cord holder through the fabric and into the lath at the marked position.

4 To fix the blind to the roller, mark a straight line alon the roller and attach a narrow strip of double-sided tape. Lay th blind right side u and place the roll across the top, with the spring mechanism to your left. Partially roll the fabric around the roller so that the fabric edge matches the tape edge; press down along the tape to hold. Attach with staples c tacks at approximately 1-inch intervals.

5 To hang the blind, first roll it up and place the roller in the brackets. Pull the blind down, then give a quick tug to release the stop, and allow it to roll up. If the spring is not fully tensioned, the blind will not roll up correctly. In this case, remove the blind, roll it up again, and repeat. This time the blind should roll up on its own.

STRAIGHT-EDGE BLIND
To create a blind with a straight lower edge, neaten the lower raw edge with zigzag stitch, then turn up a single hem wide enough to take the lath. Press the fold with your fingers and stitch across the width close to the raw edge.

Roman blind

When pulled up, a Roman blind forms neat horizontal pleats. This effect is achieved by cords threaded through rings or loops on rows of vertical tapes running across the back of the blind (see pages 58 and 59).

Before making the blind, attach the brackets at the window (see pages 60 and 61) and paint both the brackets and the furring strip to match the window frame.

MATERIALS: Closely woven cotton fabric, lining fabric, matching thread, Roman-blind tape, blind cord, screw eyes, self-adhesive hook-and-loop fastening tape, furring strip, L-shape brackets, rings, lath, cleat and screws

FABRIC: Follow the instructions for measuring the window and calculating the quantities of fabric and materials required (see pages 62 and 63).

1 Join widths of fabric, if necessary, to obtain the required blind width. Stitch the lining in the same way. Pin the fabric and lining together with right sides facing and matching the sides and top edge. Stitch together ½ inch from the raw edge on each side. (The fabric will be wider than the lining.) Press seams open and turn right side out.

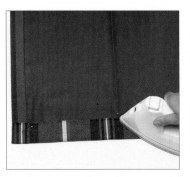

2 Use a pin to mark the center point on the lining and the fabric at the top and bottom edges. With the lining on top, align the pins, then press the side edges with an equal overlap of the top fabric on each side of the lining. Turn up the lower hem on the fabric so the hem edge sits just over the raw edge of the lining. Press, but do not stitch.

3 Working on the lining side, position a tape vertically, covering the left seam line. Place the lower edge of the tape just inside the hem edge and the first ring (loop) position just above it. Baste in place. Repeat on the opposite side, making sure the ring (loop) positions line up exactly across the blind.

4 Space the rest of the tapes at equal intervals (8½ to 11 inches apart) vertically across the blind, lining up the ring (loop) positions. (Wider intervals will cause the blind to droop.) Baste and stitch tapes down each side close to the edge. To define pleats, stitch horizontal lines across the blind at each ring (loop) position.

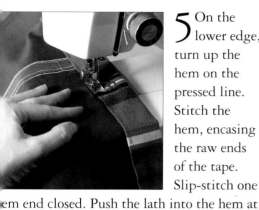

5 On the lower edge, turn up the hem on the pressed line. Stitch the hem, encasing the raw ends of the tape. Slip-stitch one

6 Zigzag-stitch fabric and lining together along the top raw edge. Press the loop strip of the self-adhesive tape flush with the top edge of the fabric and stitch in place. Press the hook strip to the front of the furring strip, flush

em end closed. Push the lath into the hem at he open end and then slip-stitch the open nd closed.

with the top edge. Press the blind in place. Mark screw eye positions on the underside of the strip, lining up the positions with each tape. Affix the screw eyes in place.

7 If looped tape is used, fix a ring to the tape just above the hem edge. Secure the cord end to the hem edge ring, then thread it through the rings (loops). At the top of the tape, thread the cord through the screw eyes on the furring strip and out to one side. Make sure all the cord lengths lie to one side of the blind. Then screw the furring strip to the brackets and attach the cleat at the side of the window to match the cords. Tie the cords together and pull up the blind.

Festoon blind

A festoon blind, which is gathered both horizontally and vertically even when it's lowered, looks best when made up in sheer or very fine fabrics.

The blind shown here is made to hang from a special blind track that comes with integral cord holders. This track is fixed to the wall in the same way as ordinary curtain track (see pages 20 and 21).

MATERIALS: Sheer fabric, transparent curtain heading tape, blind track, festoon blind tape, nylon cord, small transparent curtain rings, matching thread, cord tidy, cleat and screws

FABRIC: Follow the instructions for measuring the windows and calculating the quantities of fabric and materials required (see pages 62 and 63). If adding a ruffle, calculate the extra fabric required (see pages 84 and 85) and add this to fabric quantities.

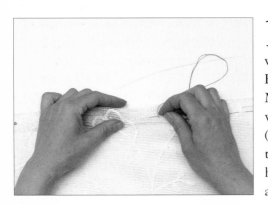

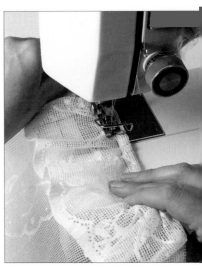

1 Make up the required width of fabric, joining widths together with French seams (see page 81). Match the design across the widths on patterned fabrics (see pages 24 and 25). Then turn under a single 1-inch hem down each side edge and baste to hold.

2 With the fabric wrong side up, pin one strip of festoon blind tape vertically over each side hem; the tape should just cover the raw edge of the fabric hem, and the first loop should lie 2 inches from the lower raw edge of the fabric. The loops along the tape should lie towards the center of the blind. Position additional vertical tape lengths in the same manner across the blind at equally spaced intervals of about 16 to 24 inches; cover seams where possible. At the bottom end of each tape, pull the cords to the back of the tape and knot to secure. Stitch each tape down the center. Attach one transparent ring to the loop near the bottom of each tape.

3 To add a ruffle, cut and piece fabric strips to make up the ruffle (see pages 84 and 85). Pull up the gathering threads evenly to fit the lower edge of the blind. With wrong sides facing, stitch the ruffle to the blind with a ¼ inch seam, catching the vertical tape ends in the seam. Turn to the right side. Refold, press, and stitch ⅜ inch from the seamed edge as for a French seam (see page 81).

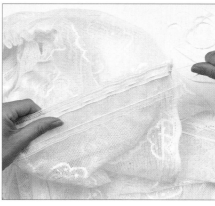

5 Draw up each vertical tape to the finished blind length and knot. Don't cut the cords; wind them around the cord tidy. Arrange the gathers evenly.

4 On the top edge, turn under a 1-inch hem to the wrong side. Place the transparent curtain heading tape ¼ inch from the top (folded) edge. Trim the top end of each vertical tape so that it will just tuck under the lower edge of the heading tape. Pull out the cords on the vertical tapes so that they hang free below the heading tape, then stitch the heading tape in position (see steps 4–6, pages 28 and 29).

Pull up the cords in the heading tape to the track width and secure. Attach hooks, evenly spaced, across the heading. Knot a length of nylon cord to the ring at the lower edge of the vertical tape on the opposite side of the blind from the cord lock. Thread the cord through the loops to the top. Leave an extra length of cord the width and length of the blind before cutting off. Continue in the same manner, threading cord through the loops on each length of tape.

6 Hang the blind from the track and thread each length of cord through the cord holder above the tape and out to the cord lock at the side. Fix the cleat on the same side of the window as the cord lock. Knot the cords together and wind around the cleat. The blind can be raised and lowered when desired.

Austrian blind

Closely woven cotton is suitable for a lined Austrian blind such as the one shown here, while fine fabrics such as lace, muslin, and voile are suitable for unlined blinds.

To make the required width, it often will be necessary to join widths of fabric. To avoid an unsightly seam down the center of the blind, stitch half widths to the sides of a central panel.

Before making the blind, install a blind track suitable for Austrian or festoon blinds at the window (see page 61). Or mount ordinary curtain track onto a furring strip (see pages 20 and 21).

MATERIALS: Furnishing fabric, lining fabric, deep pencil-pleat heading tape, blind track, Austrian blind tape and cord, small curtain rings, matching thread, curtain hooks, cleat and screws

FABRIC: Follow the instructions for measuring the windows and calculating the quantities of fabric and materials required (see pages 62 and 63).

1 Stitch lengths of fabric together with open seams to make up the required width, making sure the pattern matches across the joined lengths (see pages 24 and 25). Join widths of lining in the same manner.

2 Turn in a single 2-inch hem down each side and along the lower edge of the fabric and press. Miter the corners (see pages 82 and 83) and use large herringbone stitches to hold.

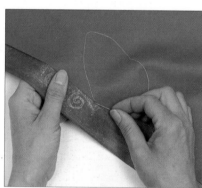

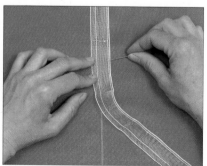

positions across the blind. Baste tapes in place, then stitch along each side edge. Turn under a ½-inch hem on the lining, with the tape ends tucked inside. Slip-stitch to the top fabric hem.

3 Place the lining right side up over the wrong side of the fabric, with 1 inch of fabric showing around each side and on the lower edge. (The space between the top edge of the fabric and the lining should equal the width of the heading tape.) Lockstitch the lining to the fabric at any seams between joined widths (see pages 38 and 39). On the sides of the lining, fold under a ½-inch hem, then slip-stitch lining in place over the side hems. Leave the lower edge free.

4 Position a length of tape over the inner edge of each side hem, with the raw tape end even with the finished edge of the lower hem. Mark vertical lines across the fabric at equally spaced intervals of about 12 to 16 inches. Pin tapes in position, centering them over each marked line and aligning loop

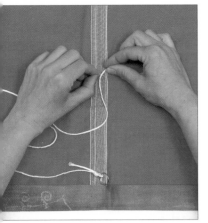

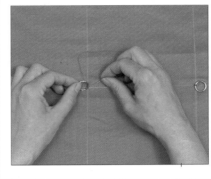

RINGS WITHOUT STITCHES

Mark vertical lines as in Step 4. Draw in horizontal lines at 6- to 9-inch intervals to within 6 inches of the top edge. Hand-stitch a ring in place where the lines intersect and also where the lines begin at the hem edges.

5 Attach the heading tape (see pages 28 and 29). Cut a length of cord and tie it to the bottom ring on the tape; thread it vertically through the loops and out to the side. Repeat for each line of tape. Gather the heading tape to fit the blind track length and secure.

6 Hang the blind, then position the cord holders and thread the cords through the holders and out to one side (see pages 60 and 61). Fix the cleat below the cord lock and pull the blind cords to ensure that the blind gathers equally across the width. When satisfied, knot the cords together and trim the ends. Pull up the blind and secure around the cleat.

Sewing Techniques

For your work to have a professional finish, you need to know how to make corners lie flat and how to finish by hand correctly. It's also helpful to know which type of seam is best for joining widths of fabric to create a sturdy seam.

This chapter explains how to work the essential hand stitches as well as how to create mitered corners and a range of different seams. It also includes instructions for making piping, ruffles, and borders, and applying decorative edgings.

This chapter contains

Essential sewing kit	76
Hand stitches	78
Seams and hems	80
Corners	82
Piping and ruffles	84
Borders	86
Finishing touches	88

Essential sewing kit

If you already enjoy sewing, most of the items here will be in your workbox. With care, good quality sewing tools will last for years, so if you need to buy new ones, choose the best you can afford. If you don't have a workbox, buy one or make one, and save yourself hours of searching for a tape measure and scissors.

MEASURING AND MARKING

Tape measure: a vital part of any sewing kit. Choose a tape measure made of nylon or some other material that will not stretch and that has metal protective ends. Each side of the tape should start and finish at opposite ends so that you do not have to unwind the tape to find the starting point.

Pencil: for copying patterns onto tracing paper. A soft pencil, such as a 2B, is the easiest to use.

Tailor's chalk: comes in several colors, but white is the easiest to remove later. Keep the edge sharp. You also can use a dressmaker's pencil, which has a brush for removing the marks from the fabric.

Steel tape: the most reliable tool for measuring furniture or windows when you are calculating the quantities of material required.

CUTTING

Cutting-out scissors: should have a 6-inch blade and be flat on one side. Never use on any other material except fabric.

Pinking shears: have a serrated blade which makes a zigzag cut. They are used to neaten raw edges, particularly on fabrics that fray easily.

Needlework scissors: are helpful for snipping threads, cutting into or notching seams, making buttonholes, and other close trimming jobs.

STITCHING

Pins: come in a wide range of sizes. Those with glass or plastic heads are the easiest to use. Have a pincushion handy to store unused pins; that way you can avoid finding them later by accident.

Needles: Keep a variety of needle types and sizes in your workbox to handle all kinds of fabric and trims. The most useful are sharps (long needles used for tacking and gathering), betweens (small, sharp needles used for hand-sewing), ball-point (used on knitted fabrics to prevent snagging), and bodkins (short, blunt needles used for threading cord and elastic through casings).

MACHINE SEWING

Sewing machines: Available in a wide range of different models, a sewing machine is a worthwhile investment that should last a lifetime. Almost all models do the basic stitches required to complete the projects in this book.

Machine needles: Choose fine needles and fine threads when working with fine fabrics, thicker needles and thicker threads for thicker fabrics.

PRESSING

You'll need a clean dry/steam iron and an ironing board. Keep a clean cloth on hand, too, for pressing delicate fabrics and for those times when you need extra steam on hard-to-press creases in natural fabrics.

THE RIGHT THREAD FOR THE JOB

Cotton: smooth, strong thread with a slight sheen. Use this on linen and all cotton fabrics.

Mercerized cotton thread: all-purpose thread, suitable for a variety of fabrics.

Cotton-wrapped polyester: The polyester provides strength while the cotton provides smoothness and luster.

Silk thread: Use for stitching silk and for basting fine fabrics by hand (because it leaves no marks).

Buttonhole twist: available in synthetic or silk. Use for topstitching as well as buttonholes.

Hand stitches

Assembling window treatments calls for hand stitches at specific stages, and the stitches create a professional finish. You'll need to know how to work the stitches shown here to make the projects in this book.

LOCKSTITCH

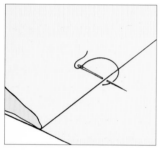

1 Lay the fabric and lining together with wrong sides facing. Pin together on the center line, vertically down the length of the fabrics. Fold back the lining to the pinned line.

Starting about 12 inches from the lower edge, secure the thread in the lining with a knot. Make a tiny stitch in the main fabric, picking up just one thread. Leave a 1-inch gap, then make a one-thread stitch from the lining back to the top fabric, working over the thread to form a simple loop.

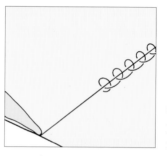

2 Continue making lockstitches every 1 inch until you reach the top edge. Keep the thread very loose so the fabric does not pucker. Unfold the fabric before smoothing the layers back together. Make another vertical row of pins 15 inches from the last vertical row. Fold back the lining and make lockstitches as before. Continue making rows of stitches across the complete width of the fabrics until the layers are joined.

LADDER STITCH

Use this method to baste two pieces of a patterned fabric together so that the pattern matches exactly across the seam. After basting, turn the fabric to the wrong side to stitch.

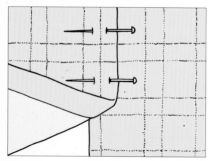

1 On the edge of one of the two pieces of fabric to be joined, press under ½ inch. Place the folded edge over the second piece, matching the raw edges and the pattern. Pin in position.

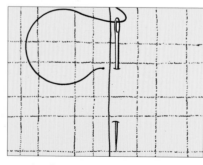

2 Anchor the thread within the fold line and take a small stitch across to the other piece of fabric. Following the fold, take a ½- to ¾-inch stitch on the underside of the fabric.

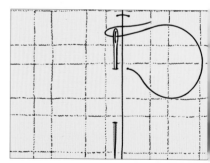

3 Take the needle straight across to the folded side of the fabric, then make another ½- to ¾-inch-long stitch inside the folded edge. Continue for the entire length of the seam.

HERRINGBONE STITCH

This is the stitch used to hold interlinings in place, but it also can be used to stitch a raw-edged hem.

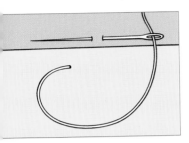

1 Baste the interlining to the fabric it is to back. Secure the thread under the interlining and bring the needle up through it. Working from left to right, take the thread diagonally to the main fabric and take a small backstitch of one to two threads in the main fabric only.

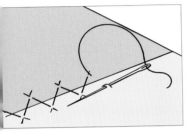

2 Still working diagonally, move across to the interlining and take another small backstitch through the interlining only. Continue in this way to the end and secure the thread in the interlining.

SLIP-STITCHING SEAMS

This is used to join two folded edges when a gap has been left in the stitching to turn an item through from the wrong to the right side.

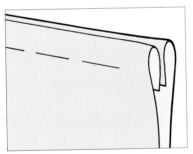

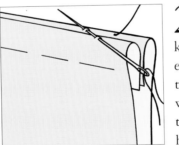

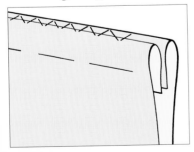

1 Fold under a narrow hem on both pieces of fabric to be joined. Baste to hold the folded edges together.

2 Hide the knotted end of the thread within the far hem and then, with folded edges held together, bring the thread into the inner side of the fold of the near hem and take a small stitch. Take a second small stitch farther along in the far hem and pull the thread.

3 Continue in this way until the opening is closed. Do not pull the thread too tight; also make sure the stitches and thread are as invisible as possible.

SLIP-STITCHING HEMS

Although machine-stitching a hem is quicker, slip-stitching creates a neater finish as the stitches are almost invisible on the right side of the fabric.

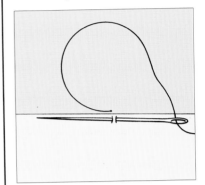

1 Fasten the thread with a knot or backstitch in the fabric of the hem and then bring the needle out on the folded edge of the hem. Pick up one thread, or at the most two, from the main fabric close to the hem edge.

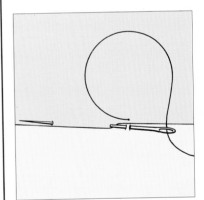

2 Take a ¾- to 1-inch-long stitch along the fold of the hem and pull the thread through. Continue in this manner, picking up a thread from the main fabric and taking a long stitch along the hem edge until the hem is completely stitched.

Seams and hems

Machine-stitched seams and hems are tough and durable. There are several types of seams from which to choose, ranging from a simple open seam to enclosed seams, such as flat-fell and French seams.

ZIGZAG STITCH

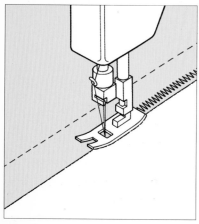

A machine zigzag stitch is commonly used to neaten the raw edges of the seam allowance on open seams that won't be covered. Set the machine for a short and narrow zigzag and stitch along each raw edge of the allowance, slightly in from the edge. Trim the edge just short of the stitches. On fabrics that fray badly, use a wider stitch.

TOPSTITCHED HEM

A topstitched hem worked on a machine provides a strong result in a minimum amount of time. Because it shows more than a hand-stitched hem, it can also be a decorative element.

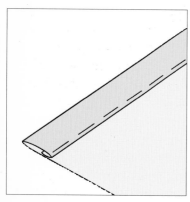

1 Press under a single narrow hem to the wrong side. Then turn the hem to the required width, forming a double hem. Baste in position.

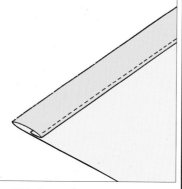

2 Working from the wrong side of the fabric, machine-stitch the hem close to the inner folded edge.

OPEN SEAM

This is the seam most commonly used to stitch two lengths of fabric together. It is used for all main seams on curtains and blinds when the raw edges will be covered by a lining.

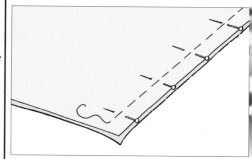

1 With the right sides facing, pin the two pieces of fabric together ½ inch from the raw edges. Baste just inside the seam line, if basting is considered necessary.

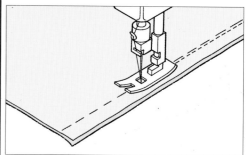

2 Set the machine to reverse. Starting ½ inch from the end, stitch back to the start on the seam line. Then stitch forward, removing any pins as you work. Finish by reverse stitching.

FLAT-FELL SEAM

The raw edge of a flat-fell seam is encased within the seam, but, unlike a French seam, both lines of stitching appear on the surface. This makes it a tough seam and ideal for use on furnishings that must be regularly laundered, such as bedding and table linens. Here the stitching is done on the back of the fabric. However, it also can be done on the front.

FRENCH SEAMS

A French seam is really two seams, one enclosed within the other. The raw edges are contained within the finished seam, giving a tough fray-free finish on the wrong side. It is a neat, narrow seam that is ideal for use on sheer fabrics.

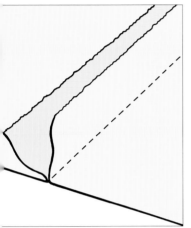

1 With the right sides together, match up the raw edges of the fabric pieces. Pin, baste, and then stitch ½ inch from the raw edge.

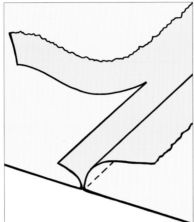

2 Press to one side. Then trim the seam allowance on the underside of the seam to a scant ¼ inch.

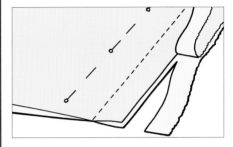

1 With the wrong sides together, match the raw edges of the pieces of fabric to be joined. Pin, then stitch ¼ inch outside the finished seam line. If necessary, trim close to stitched line.

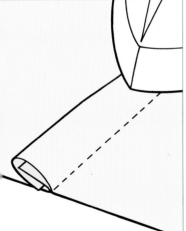

3 Press the wider seam allowance in half with the narrower allowance encased inside. Then press the seam down to the back of the fabric.

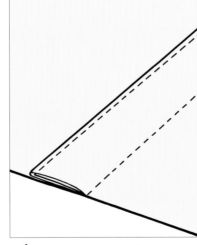

4 Pin the seam in place and baste to hold it secure while you work. Then machine-stitch the seam close to the folded edge.

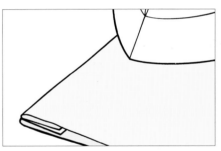

2 Press the seam flat, then turn the fabric so the right sides of the fabric are facing with this first seam line on the edge. Press well.

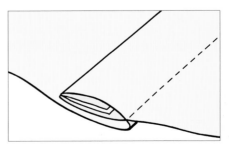

3 Baste, then stitch along the finished seam line. Press.

Corners

Neat, crisp corners give a project a professional look, but to achieve this effect, you need to take a little extra care with some special stitching and trimming.

To make corners less bulky, miter them, cutting away any excess fabric. A similar effect can be achieved by simply folding the excess fabric into the miters to create mock miters. Folding miters, rather than cutting them, is a practical choice if you might need to lower the curtain hems later.

MOCK MITER

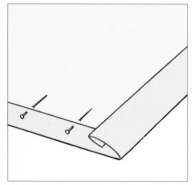

1 A mock miter is used to reduce bulk on corners without cutting away fabric. Turn in and press double hems along the sides and bottom of the fabric; pin in place.

2 Fold in the bottom hem or the diagonal so that the fold meets the inner side hem edge and looks like a miter. Slip-stitch the corner fold in place to secure.

STITCHING CORNERS

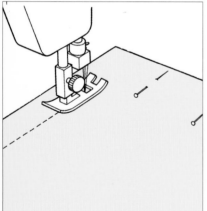

1 To get a sharp angle when stitching a corner, stop one stitch away from the corner and do the last stitch slowly, using the hand wheel if necessary. Leave the needle down in the fabric.

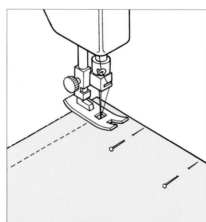

2 Raise the foot and turn the fabric. Then lower the foot and continue stitching. To give the corner extra strength, use a shorter stitch just before and after the corner.

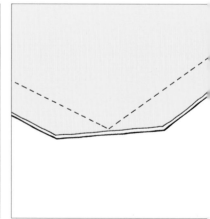

3 Trim the fabric diagonally across the corner just outside the corner point. This ensures that the corner will lie flat when turned to the right side.

MITERING AN EVEN HEMMED CORNER

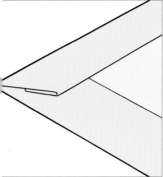

1 On the side and lower edges of the fabric, press under a single hem to the wrong side. Then turn under a second hem to make a double hem. Press well, so that the fold lines for the hems are clear.

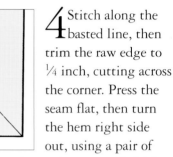

2 Open out the second hem fold and refold the fabric diagonally so the fold runs across the corner point of the second hem fold. Press this fold, then open out all pressed edges.

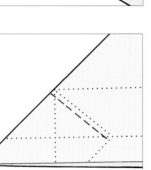

3 With the right sides of the fabric facing, fold the fabric on the diagonal at the corner, with the angled fold lines aligned. Baste ¼ inch outside this fold line to the first (single-hem) fold line only.

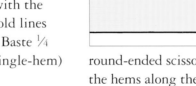

4 Stitch along the basted line, then trim the raw edge to ¼ inch, cutting across the corner. Press the seam flat, then turn the hem right side out, using a pair of round-ended scissors to push out the corner. Refold the hems along the pressed lines and slip-stitch.

MITERING AN UNEVEN HEMMED CORNER

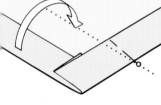

1 Press under a single hem (Step 1, above). Press in a double hem on what will be the narrower edge. Mark with a pin where the hem edge meets the lower pressed hem edge.

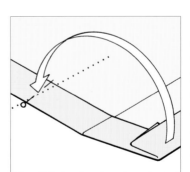

2 Open out and then repeat with the wider hem, marking the point where it meets the narrower hem edge.

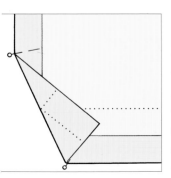

3 Unfold the second part of the hem only and, with single hems in position, press the corner fabric diagonally from one pin mark to the other.

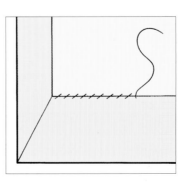

4 Then either trim the corner fabric (see steps 3 and 4 above) or replace the double hems and slip-stitch the mitered corner without removing any corner fabric.

Piping and ruffles

Piping creates a neat finish on an edge or seam. It can be made with piping cord sandwiched between the fabric to form a smooth, rounded edge or made without the cord for a flat piping.

Single and double ruffles are simple to make and can be attached to curtains, blinds, and tiebacks to give them a more elaborate finish.

PIPING

To work out the fabric requirements, measure all the edges to be piped. Add 2 inches for every join to give the total length of fabric strips and piping required. When buying cotton piping cord, allow for shrinkage and wash the cord before using it. Cut fabric for piping on the bias.

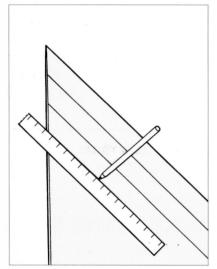

1 Lay fabric flat with the selvages at the sides; remove the selvages. Fold over a top corner on the diagonal and press. With a dressmaker's pencil, draw lines parallel to the fabric fold at 2-inch intervals. Cut the fabric strips. To make a continuous length, pin the fabric strips together along the straight grain of the fabric and with right sides facing. Stitch together with narrow seams. Trim the seams and press open.

2 With the wrong sides facing, fold the fabric strip in half lengthwise and encase the piping cord in it. Pin, then use a zipper foot to stitch along the strip close to the cord. To apply, stitch the piping to the right side of one piece of fabric, matching raw edges and placing the piping stitching line over the fabric seam line. Begin stitching ½ inch from the piping end.

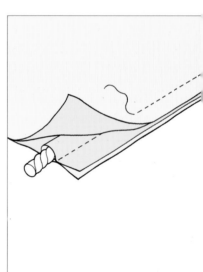

3 To join the ends, stop stitching 2 inches before the end. Trim the cord ends to meet, leaving a ½-inch overlap of piping fabric. Turn the overlap under ¼ inch. Wrap around the cord ends and stitch across the join. To finish the project, layer the second piece of fabric over the piped stitching line, with right sides facing and raw edges aligned. Stitch along the seam line. Turn right side out and press.

[SI]NGLE RUFFLE

[T]he depth of the ruffle depends on the furnishing to which it is to be attached. As a rough guide, choose a [d]epth between 2½ and 4 inches. Then add seam and hem allowances. Measure the length of the edges [to] which the ruffle is to be added and double this measurement for the ruffle length.

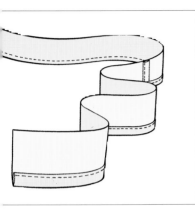

1 Remove the selvages from the fabric. On the wrong side of the fabric, mark the ruffle strips to the determined depth across the full width [of] the fabric, using a dressmaker's pencil. Cut [en]ough strips to make up the complete ruffle. Join [th]e strips together with narrow French seams (see [p]age 81). On one long edge, turn under a double [½]-inch hem to the wrong side and stitch in place. [R]epeat for the short ends.

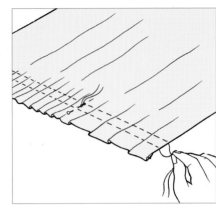

2 Using the longest machine stitch, run two rows of gathering threads along the raw edge. Stitch in sections of about 24 inches.

Backstitch at one end to secure and leave a length of thread at the opposite end for pulling up. Gather the ruffle evenly to fit the fabric edge. To secure the gathers, wind the thread ends around pins. With the raw edges together and right sides facing, baste, then stitch in position. Neaten the raw edges.

[D]OUBLE RUFFLE

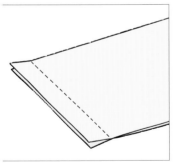

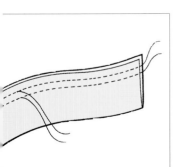

1 Estimate the length of fabric required for a double ruffle in the same way as for the single ruffle, but allow twice the depth plus 1 inch (for ½-inch seam allowances). Join the strips with open seams, then fold in half lengthwise with the right sides facing. Stitch the ends to secure. For a continuous ruffle, join ends together.

2 Turn the fabric strip right side out. Refold and press. Stitch rows of gathering threads through both layers along the raw edge (see Single Ruffle, above), pulling up the threads in the same way. Baste the ruffle to the main fabric with right sides facing and raw edges matching. Stitch in place before neatening the raw edges.

BINDING RAW EDGES

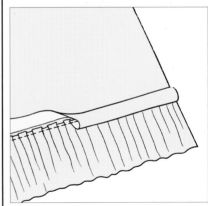

For a neat, bound edge, allow a seam allowance of 1½ inches on the main fabric only. When the ruffle has been stitched in place, encase the ruffle raw edge with the wide main fabric edge. Tuck under ½ inch, then slip-stitch or machine-stitch in place.

Borders

A border acts like a frame, giving the edge of a curtain, blind, or valance definition. It can be used to link the window treatment visually with other furnishings in the room. It's also a clever way of enlarging curtains or blinds for use in a new setting.

A plain border can be made as a complete frame or attached to the sides and the lower edge only. On curtains, a border can be stitched to the leading and lower edges only.

An applied edging strip, cut to the outline of a fabric's motif, adds a decorativ finish to the plain edge of a roller blind or a shaped valance. It also can be used t coordinate a ready-made blind with the curtains or other furnishings in the room

APPLIED DECORATIVE BORDER

Choose fabric with a bold motif that is easy to cut around. You will need a strip of fabric the chosen dept by the width of the edge to which it is to be attached. If the border is to be attached to a blind, it will be necessary to make a new pocket for the lath above where the border is to be attached, since the lower edg of the applied border will sit just within the lower edge of the blind. Remove the lath, remove the stitche in the existing casing, then make a new casing (see Step 3, page 66). When applying a border to unstiffened fabric, outline the motifs with satin stitch after joining the two fabrics; this prevents fraying.

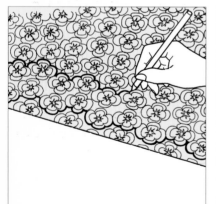

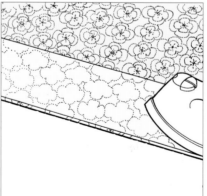

1 Decide on the length and width of the border required, then mark this on the border fabric. Draw around the outline of the motifs on the right side of the fabric, using a dressmaker's pencil or chalk.

2 Cut a strip of double-sided iron-on interfacing slightly larger than the motif area and place it on the wrong side of the border fabric. Peel off the backing paper and press in place. Cut out the border following the outline.

3 Place the border just inside the shaped-valance or blind lower edge on the right side of the fabric, matching the side edges. Press the border in place. Trim the lower edge following the border outline.

DOUBLE BORDER

A double border is a piece of folded fabric which is attached to the main fabric at the front and the back, with the raw edges of the main fabric sandwiched between the two halves of the border strip. When you use this type of border, you don't need to add a hem allowance to the fabric for the curtain or blind.

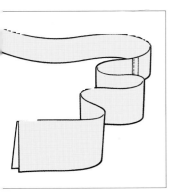

1 First measure each raw edge to which the border is to be attached. Add 1 inch (for ½-inch seam allowances) to the length measurement of each border piece. Decide on the border width required; double this measurement and add 1 inch (for ½-inch seam allowances). Using these measurements, cut out the border pieces. Join the fabric where necessary to make the required lengths. Cut separate borders for each side.

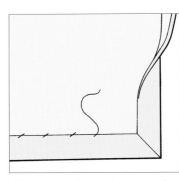

2 Press each border piece in half lengthwise with the wrong sides facing. Where border pieces are to join at right angles, create a diagonal on each piece by folding each corner of the raw short edge over to the fold. Press to mark the fold then trim ½ inch outside the diagonal fold line. Open out. With the right sides facing, stitch corners together along the diagonal fold lines. Press and turn right side out. Fold into an L-shaped border and press.

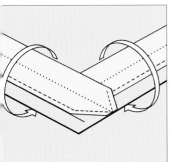

3 Sandwich the main fabric inside the border pieces, with raw edges matching border folds. Lightly mark the border's raw edge on the right side. Remove the border and draw a second line 1 inch outside the first. Replace the border lower edge with right sides of fabrics matching. Align the border raw edge with the second drawn line, with a mitered inner corner on any corner point. Stitch lower edge. Repeat for side edges. Turn in any short raw ends and slip-stitch closed.

4 Press, then turn the border over the end of the fabric, sandwiching the main fabric between the border. Press under a ½-inch seam allowance along the raw edge of the back border and baste in place on the wrong side of the fabric. Slip-stitch in place, following the stitching line on the front border edge.

USING A BORDER TO INCREASE THE FABRIC SIZE

When a border is used to increase the size of a curtain or a blind, the border pieces need to be cut to fit its finished size, rather than its existing size. Work out the length required for the side border pieces, and add the border depth measurement to the side measurement of the curtain or blind. For the lower border piece, add twice the border depth measurement to the lower edge measurement. Attach the border to the main fabric, positioning it with right sides facing and raw edges matching.

Finishing touches

Making neat seams can be very satisfying, but that doesn't mean you always have to leave them visible. Braid, cord, and ribbon can all be used to decorate the finished project, and using coordinating colors can do much to enhance your color scheme.

BRAID

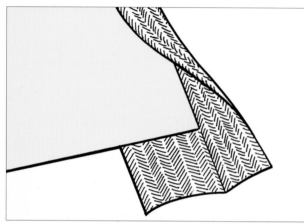

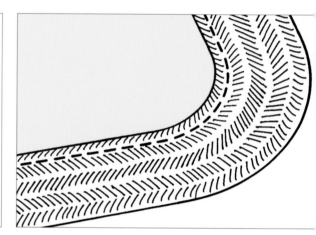

1 Apply fold-over braid. With the narrower edge on the fabric's right side, baste both layers in place through the fabric.

2 Topstitch from the right side close to the edge. This also catches the slightly wider band of braid on the wrong side.

NARROW BRAID

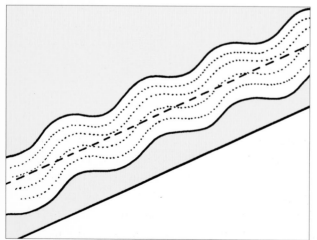

Narrow braid such as rickrack can be attached with a single line of topstitching down the center.

FRINGE

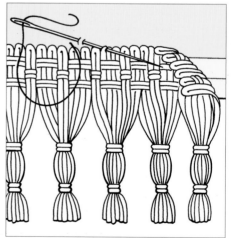

When applying fringe to the lower edge of curtains or blinds, begin by turning a narrow hem to the right side of the fabric. Then baste the braid edge of the fringe in place over this hem and machine-stitch in position.

ORD

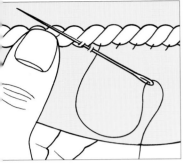

1 If the cord is not to be attached to the edge of the fabric, mark the line it is to follow

with tailor's chalk or basting stitches. Stitch the cord in place using slip-stitches and a thread that matches the background fabric. Use your other hand to hold the cord in position as you work.

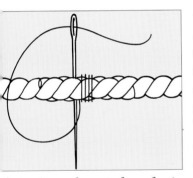

2 To join cord, allow ½ inch at each end for joining. Trim one end and dot with

fabric glue to keep it from fraying. Allow to dry. Trim the other end, apply a dot of glue, then press it to the end of the first length. Allow the glue to dry, then slip-stitch the new length in position. To disguise the join, cover it by wrapping it with closely spaced stitches of matching thread.

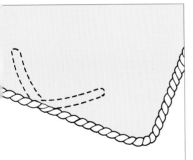

3 If the join meets over a seam, insert both cord ends in the seam. Close the seam

and slip-stitch the cords together on the top edge to form a continuous line.

RIBBON

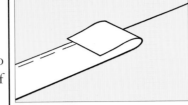

When applying ribbon, first mark where it is to go with tailor's chalk. Baste the ribbon in place over the marked line. When applying satin ribbon, which shows stitch marks, baste close to the edges. To attach the ribbon, topstitch down each side, using a straight stitch. Or, use zigzag or decorative embroidery stitches over the edges of the ribbon.

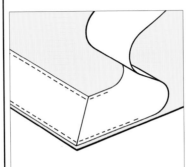

When applying ribbon along the edge of fabric, turn the hem on the fabric to the wrong side to the width of the ribbon. Line up the ribbon with the hem edge, mitering at the corners. Machine-stitch in place along each side.

CURTAIN FINISHING TIPS

• Because heavy curtains may drop slightly when hung, altering the level of the hem, hang them up for a few days before stitching the hem. Include curtain weights in the hem so the curtains hang well.

• On curtains or blinds, use a cord tidy to contain the pulled-up heading cords neatly at the outside edge of the curtain. You also can wind the cords around your hand to create a neat bundle, then tie together with a plastic-bag twist closure. Doing this makes it easier to stretch the tape flat before laundering or dry cleaning the curtains or blinds.

• After hanging curtains, draw them back and arrange them in neat folds. Then loosely tie them in place with strips of fabric at the top, bottom, and center. Leave for a couple of days to let the folds "set" before removing the ties. In the same way, raise Roman blinds to the top of the window. Arrange and press the pleats in place with your hands; let them set for a few days.

CORD-TRIMMED TIEBACK
Pages 44 and 45

SCALLOP-EDGE TIEBACK
Page 45

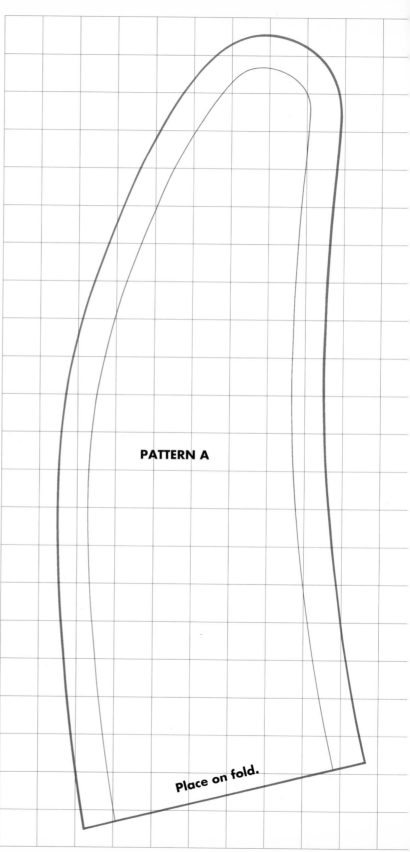

PATTERN A

Place on fold.

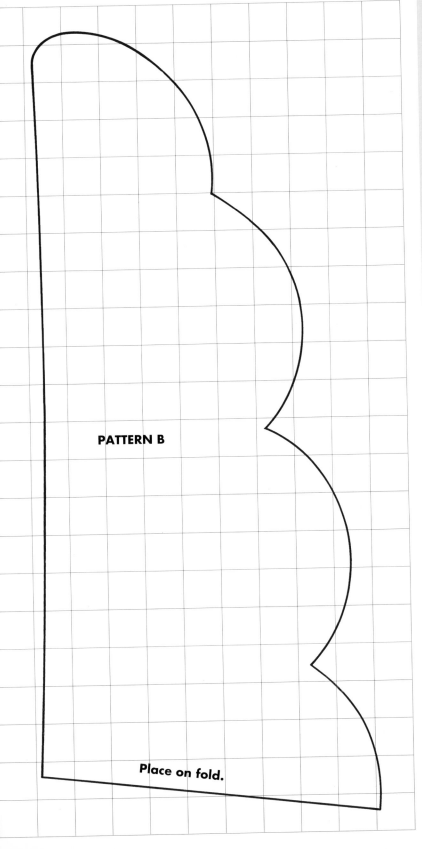

PATTERN B

Place on fold.

ENLARGING

The tieback patterns on these pages are one-half of their actual size and must be enlarged before use. The simplest way to do this is to enlarge them by 200% on a photocopier with an enlargement capability.

To enlarge them by hand, draw a grid on paper increasing the ³/₈-inch squares shown here in proportion to the size required. For example, to increase the template 200%, draw a grid with ³/₄-inch squares. Then, draw in the pattern, one square at a time, creating the scaled-up version on the larger squared grid. Using these methods you can enlarge and reduce the templates.

Glossary

Basting
A temporary stitch to hold fabrics in position and act as a guide for permanent stitching.

Bias
A diagonal angle to the straight weft and warp threads of a fabric. Strips cut on the bias are used for piping and binding, because they stretch and can be applied around a curve without puckering.

Clipping
Making snips at regular intervals into the seam allowance. This allows the fabric to stretch and give where necessary when it is turned to the right side.

Double hem
When fabric is folded twice so that the raw edge is hidden within the hem.

Flat-fell seam
A sturdy seam in which the raw edge is encased within the seam and both lines of stitching appear on the surface. Ideal for use on furnishings that are laundered regularly.

Flush window
A window that is level with the surface of the wall on all sides. Curtains and blinds for flush windows are usually made larger than the window size.

French seam
A neat, narrow seam which is really two seams, one enclosed within the other. Ideal for use on sheer fabrics.

Grain
The direction in which the fibers run in a length of fabric.

Interfacing
Special material, available in sew-on or iron-on forms, which is attached to the wrong side of the main fabric to provide stiffness, shape, and support.

Interlining
An extra layer of fabric, placed between the main fabric and lining, to add insulation, thickness, and weight.

Iron-on
The term used to describe the chemical reaction when one fabric (usually interfacing) is fused to another with a warm iron.

Ladder stitch
The professional method used to baste two pieces of a patterned fabric together so that the pattern matches across the seam.

Lath
A thin strip of wood that is slotted inside a pocket in the fabric of a blind and used to hold the fabric flat along its lower edge.

Miter
Used on a corner between two right-angled sides to give a neat, angled join that does away with surplus fabric.

Motif
The dominant element in a fabric design.

Notching
Making V-shape cuts into the seam allowance to a point just outside the seam. This is used on a sharply curved seam to ensure the seam allowance lies flat when the fabric is turned to the right side.

pen seam

he simplest way to join two
eces of fabric together. Fabrics
e placed right sides together,
achine-stitched along a seam
ne parallel to the fabric raw
lge, and then pressed open.
sed where a lining will cover
e seam and hide any raw edges.
lso known as a flat seam.

attern repeat

fabric with a repeating pattern,
e depth of one complete design
a length of fabric.

ecessed window

window that is set back from
e wall surface.

eam allowance

he area between the seam line
nd the raw edge. On fabric that
ays easily, the seam allowance
eeds to be neatened and secured
ith zigzag stitches.

Seam line

The line designated for stitching
the seam.

Selvage

The plain, woven edge along each
side of the fabric. It prevents
raveling and should be cut off
before the fabric is cut out.

Single hem

When fabric is folded once, either
to the front or back, so that the
raw edge is exposed. A single
hem usually is used when the
hem will be covered by another
piece of fabric.

Slip-stitch

An almost invisible stitch used
for securing hems or joining two
folded edges on the right side of
the fabric.

Straight grain

Follows the warp threads, which
run down the length of the fabric
parallel to the selvages.

Tension

On a sewing machine, the balance
and tightness of the needle and
bobbin threads, which combine
to create the perfect stitch.

Topstitch

A line of stitching on the right
side of the fabric, often used as
a decorative highlight.

Valance shelf

A narrow shelf with a front edge
from which a shaped valance
hangs. The width of the shelf
holds the valance fabric away from
the curtains or blind behind it.

Warp

Parallel threads running
lengthwise down woven fabric,
interlacing with the weft threads.

Weft

Threads that run from side to side
across woven fabric, interlacing
with the warp threads.

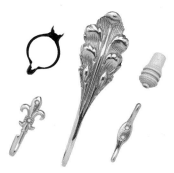

Index

archway drape 53
Austrian blinds 25, 59
  fabric quantity 63
  making 72–73
  track 12, 61

basting 93
bathrooms 7, 9, 28, 58
bay windows 7, 12, 16
bias 84, 92
blinds
  Austrian 12, 25, 59, 61, 63, 72–73
  fabric quantity 62–63
  festoon 7, 8, 12, 17, 25, 59, 61, 62, 70–71
  hanging 60–61
  roller 9, 11, 17, 52, 58, 60, 63, 66–67, 86
  Roman 7, 11, 17, 52, 58, 61, 63, 68–69, 89
  styles 58–59
borders 16, 17, 48, 58, 86–87
bound edges 85
box pleats 19
braid 88
buttons 11, 35, 39

café curtains 7, 13, 27, 34–35
calico 9
cased headings 32–33
cleaning 8, 22, 28, 89
clipping 44, 92
cord tidy 11, 61, 70, 89
cords 16, 44–45, 89
corners 75, 82–83, 89
cotton fabrics 8, 9, 10
creasing 8, 9, 22, 89
curtain clips 11, 53

curtains
  borders 86–87
  dressing 42–55
  finishing 88–89
  lined 36–39
  setting 89
  styles 6–7, 16–17
  unlined 28–29, 40

detachable lining 12, 19, 30–31
draped headings 52–53

equipment 76–77
eyelet kits 11

fabric
  estimating quantity 23, 62–63
  joining widths 25, 28, 36, 63, 72
  pattern 16, 22, 24–25, 36, 63
  preparation 24
  safety and wear 22
  types 8–9
festoon blinds 7, 8, 25, 59
  fabric quantity 62
  fabric types 17
  making 70–71
  track 12, 61
finishing 75, 88–89
flat-fell seam 28, 34, 81, 92
floor-draped curtains 6, 16
flush window 62, 92
French seam 70, 81, 92
fringes 16, 59, 88

gingham 9
goblet pleats 19, 39
grain 24, 92, 93

heading
  attaching tape 28–29, 33
  cased 32–33
  draped 52–53
  estimating tape quantity 23
  scalloped 34, 40–41
  styles 18–19
  tabbed 34–35
  tiebacks 46
  valances 48–49
hems
  checking length 29, 37, 89
  double 29, 34, 92
  mitered corners 82, 83
  single 93
  stitching 79–80
herringbone stitch 79
hook-and-loop fastening tape 11, 51, 69

insulation 10, 36, 38, 57
interfacing 34, 44, 92
interlining 10, 38–39, 79, 92
iron-on 92
ironing 24, 77

kitchens 7, 9, 28, 58

lace 8, 17, 34
ladder stitch 28, 78, 92
large windows 6, 7, 16
lath 92
lead weights 11, 89
lead-weight tape 39
linen union 9
lining
  blinds 72
  curtains 36–39
  detachable 12, 19, 30–31
  fasteners 31

tape 19
types 10
ockstitch 38, 39, 78

measuring 23, 62–63, 76
mitered corners 82–83, 89, 92
motif 22, 25, 63, 92
muslin 8, 17, 72

natural fibers 8
needles 77
notching 41, 92

open seam 80, 93

pattern 16, 34
  matching 25, 28
  repeat 22, 93
patterns 90–91
pelmet 50
  former 11
pencil 76
pencil-pleat tape 18
pins 77
piping 84
poles 13
  draped 52–53
  mounting 20–21
  position 6, 7, 23
pressing 24, 77

radiators 17
recessed windows 7, 12, 17,
  62, 93
ribbon 40, 89
rods 13, 32, 34
roller blinds 58
  borders 86
  draped headings 52
  fabric quantity 63

fabric type 9, 17
  hanging 60
  kits 11, 60
  making 66–67
Roman blinds 7, 58
  attaching 11, 69
  draped headings 52
  fabric quantity 63
  fabric type 17
  hanging 61
  making 68–69
  setting pleats 89
ruffles 59, 70, 84, 85

scalloped heading 34, 40–41
scissors 76
screws, installing 20
seam allowance 93
seam line 93
seams 75, 79, 80–81
selvages 24, 93
sewing machine 77, 93
  hems 80
  seams 80–81
sewing techniques 75–89
sheer blinds 7, 70–71
sheer curtains 27
  hanging 8, 13, 17
  making 32–33
  smocked 19
sheer fabrics 8, 53, 59, 70, 81
shrinkage 8, 9, 22, 30, 84
single curtains 6, 7
slip-stitch 79, 93
small windows 6, 16, 34
smocked headings 19, 46
stitches 78–80
styles 6–7, 16–17, 58–59
swags and tails 16, 43, 54–55
synthetic fibers 8

tab kits 11, 35
tabbed heading 34–35
tailor's chalk 76
tall windows 17
tape measure 76
tension 93
thread 77
tiebacks 43, 44–47
topstitch 80, 93
tracks 12
  blinds 12, 61, 70, 72
  installing 20–21
  position 6, 7, 16, 23
triple-pleat tape 18

unlined curtains 28–29, 40

valance 16, 17, 43
  hanging 11, 12
  making 48–51
  smocked 19
velvet 9
voile 8, 34, 72

warp 93
washing 8, 9, 22, 28, 89
weft 93
window treatments 6–7, 16–17
wires, stretched 13, 32

zigzag stitch 80

Meredith® Press
An imprint of Meredith® Books

Do-It-Yourself Decorating
Step-by-Step Window Treatments
Editor: Vicki L. Ingham
Technical Editor: Laura H. Collins
Contributing Designer: Jeff Harrison
Copy Chief: Angela K. Renkoski
Electronic Production Coordinator: Paula Forest
Editorial and Design Assistants: Barbara A. Suk, Jennifer Norris, Karen Schirm
Production Director: Douglas M. Johnston
Production Manager: Pam Kvitne
Assistant Prepress Manager: Marjorie J. Schenkelberg

Meredith® Books
Editor in Chief: James D. Blume
Design Director: Matt Strelecki
Managing Editor: Gregory H. Kayko
Executive Editor, Shelter Books: Denise L. Caringer

Director, Sales & Marketing, Retail: Michael A. Peterson
Director, Sales & Marketing, Special Markets: Rita McMullen
Director, Sales & Marketing, Home & Garden Center Channel: Ray Wolf
Director, Operations: Valerie Wiese
Vice President, General Manager: Jamie L. Martin

Meredith Publishing Group
President, Publishing Group: Christopher M. Little
Vice President, Consumer Marketing & Development: Hal Oringer
Meredith Corporation
Chairman and Chief Executive Officer: William T. Kerr
Chairman of the Executive Committee: E.T. Meredith III

Cover photograph: George Wright
First published 1998 by Haynes Publishing
Sparkford, Nr Yeovil, Somerset BA22 7JJ, UK

All of us at Meredith® Books are dedicated to providing you with information and ideas you
need to enhance your home. We welcome your comments and suggestions about this book on
Window Treatments. Write to us at: Meredith® Books, Do-It-Yourself Editorial Department,
RW–206, 1716 Locust St., Des Moines, IA 50309–3023.